Observing Children in the Primary Classroom

Also from Unwin Hyman:

The Behaviourist in the Classroom
edited by Kevin Wheldall

Classroom Control
Martyn Denscombe

Positive Teaching: The Behavioural Approach
Kevin Wheldall and Frank Merrett

Education in Recession
Eric Hewton

Home and School
J. Goodnow and A. Burns

Teaching Art to Young Children 4-9
Rob Barnes

Understanding Educational Aims
Colin Wringe

By the same author:

Look-out (with Gordon T. Taylor) Harrap, 1974: The use of film in English teaching

Occasions, Longman, 1976: a series of thematic books on Births, Weddings, Funerals and Moments of Truth, with accompanying slide sets and notes and a students' Study Guide

On Your Marks: Beginning Secondary School Teaching, Temple Smith, 1980

Every Birmingham Teacher: Resources Guide, Westhill College, 1981

Teaching English to All, Cassell, 1987

Choices, (with Jean Mills and Les Stringer) OUP, 1985: an English course book for 14-16-year-olds

More Choices (with Jean Mills and Les Stringer) OUP, 1988

OBSERVING CHILDREN IN THE PRIMARY CLASSROOM
ALL IN A DAY
SECOND EDITION

RICHARD W. MILLS
Newman and Westhill Colleges, Birmingham

London
UNWIN HYMAN
Boston   Sydney   Wellington

Published by the Academic Division of
Unwin Hyman Ltd
15/17 Broadwick Street, London W1V 1FP

Unwin Hyman, Inc.
8 Winchester Place, Winchester, Mass. 01890, USA

Allen & Unwin (Australia) Ltd,
8 Napier Street, North Sydney, NSW 2060, Australia

Allen & Unwin (New Zealand) Ltd in association with
the Port Nicholson Press Ltd,
60 Cambridge Terrace, Wellington, New Zealand

First published in 1980 as *Classroom Observation of Primary School Children*.
This revised second edition, 1988.

British Library Cataloguing in Publication Data

Mills, Richard W. (Richard William), *1938–*
    Observing children in the primary classroom: all in a day.—2nd ed.
    1. England. Primary schools. Students. Case studies
    I. Title II. Mills, Richard W. (Richard William), *1938–*
Classroom observation of primary school children
372.18'092'6
ISBN 0-04-445176-8

Library of Congress Cataloging-in-Publication Data

Mills, Richard W.
    Observing children in the primary classroom : all in a day /
    Richard W. Mills. — 2nd ed.
        p.   cm.
    Rev. ed. of: Classroom observation of primary school children. 1980.
    Bibliography: p.
    Includes indexes.
ISBN 0-04-445176-8
    1. Observation (Educational method)—Case studies. 2. Teaching–
–Case studies. 3. Education, Elementary—England—Case studies.
I. Mills, Richard W.   Classroom observation of primary school
children. II. Title.
LB1027.28.M55 1988   88-16847
372.92'2—dc 19   CIP

Typeset in 10 on 11 point Garamond
Printed in Great Britain by
Billing and Sons Ltd, London and Worcester

Contents

Acknowledgements

First, I would like to thank the boys and girls, teachers and headteachers who feature in these pages, for their co-operation in allowing themselves and their schools to be observed in the first place. Their anonymity has been protected but, as my former headmaster used to say (albeit of wrong-doers, in his case) 'they know who they are'.

Secondly, I wish to acknowledge the help of all those who provided material for the Sequels. In some cases, they generously allowed published material to be quoted at length, and in this respect I wish to mention: Garth Read, author of *How do I Teach R.E.?* (Mary Glasgow Publications, 1986); Liz Waterland, author of *Read With Me*; Nancy Chambers of the Thimble Press; Clive Davies, of Northborough Primary School, Peterborough, for their kind permission to reproduce part of the booklet for parents, *Helping Your Child to Read*; Ian Petrie and the Special Educational Needs National Advisory Council, for extracts from the leaflet 'Developing the curriculum for children with special educational needs, the professional challenge for teachers in mainstream schools'; Barrie Wade for extracts from 'Story at home and school' *Educational Review*, Birmingham University, 1984; Rachel Gregory, author of *Assembly*, Bedfordshire Education Service, 1985; and Lorna Ridgway, author of *The Task of the Teacher in the Primary School*, Ward Lock Educational, 1976.

In other cases, authors of Sequels generated material specifically for this book. These include: my colleagues Roy Cook ('Theories of learning'), Keith Barker ('Suggested fiction'), Mary Comber ('Primary science'), and my wife, Jean, ('Teaching English to Bilingual Children').

My thanks, also, to other colleagues who answered requests for information: Bob Birch, David Flint, Shirley Mercer, Geoff Platt, Hugh Wilcock and Nigel Woodhead.

Finally, my thanks are due to Jane Harris-Matthews, Editor at Unwin Hyman, for originally proposing the revision of the book published in 1980 by Allen & Unwin, *Classroom Observation of Primary School Children*, and to Gill Barrett, Robert Fisher and Tessa Roberts for offering suggestions regarding the revision. None can be held responsible for the final product.

This new book contains substantially the same amount of observation material, day by day, but has been restructured and brought up to date with current references, new Sequels and Teacher Training Tasks, to provide plenty of data for school-based In-Service training and College-Polytechnic-University-based Initial-Training.

R.W.M.

Observing Children in the Primary Classroom

Setting the Scene

A Very Short Play

Act I

Location: A primary school somewhere in England.
Actors: A teacher and thirty children, including John.
Action: A maths class is in progress.
Three masked raiders enter and demand the dinner money. Swift Kung-Fu-type blows from the deputy head render them helpless and they are carried off. Maths continues, with estimates first, then calculations, on the amount of money the thieves might have stolen. Lightning strikes the weather cock on the school roof. It crashes through the ceiling, scattering debris about the room. When the dust settles, the children sweep away the rubbish and then write about the experience in their daily diary.
During dinner time, a mad dog, foaming at the mouth, rushes around the dining room, savaging one of the infant's dolls. The art lesson in the afternoon captures the incident in paint, clay and collage.
Then, relaxation at the end of the day with the book, *Fearsome Frankenstein Fables*.
The bell sounds. Home time.

Act II

Actors: John and his mother at home.

1

Action: Mother: What happened in school today, dear?
          John: Oh, nothing.

Curtain

It is the mother's question that I have tried to answer in this book. I can record nothing quite so dramatic as the incidents just mentioned but, for those prepared to read on, there is mention of blood and tears, a dead man, a princess, Father Christmas, cannibalism, and The Boy Who Had No Pulse.

Each chapter tells of one day in the school life of the boy or girl whose name is the chapter title. Mike is a lively, extrovert 5-year-old gypsy boy in the reception class of a small rural Church of England school. Rashda is a 6-year-old girl, with little command of English, in a multi-ethnic urban setting. David is a rather slow 7-year-old who needs very sensitive teaching at his city centre school. Lucy, a very sharp Roman Catholic 8-year-old is outstanding in all she does. Lorraine, a member of the silent majority of 9-year-olds, is a quiet self-effacing girl in a suburban junior school. And Peter, aged 10, generates his own motivation in a semi-open-plan setting.

Another day, another boy or girl, another school, another observer, and everything might have been very different. So no unwarranted grand conclusions about the state of education should be drawn from these pages. The book is not a research report, but a microcosm of the educational scene. As such, its place lies in classroom interaction literature of the 'open-ended' rather than 'pre-ordained schedule' variety. There is some balance, I hope, in the selection, which was not random. The boys and girls are from differing backgrounds, have differing interests and different educational attainments. The schools from which they come are inner ring, suburban, and rural; small and large; church and state. The teachers are like you and I. Thus, the boys and girls, schools and teachers are neither representative nor untypical.

My intention in observing them has been to record events as accurately and honestly as I can, but any classroom observer is constantly bombarded by a range of changing phenomena and, like a television camera-operator, must make some selection. What some might regard as trivial data is juxtaposed with more weighty matter, as befits a classroom. In any event, who determines what is trivial?

The focus of my attention is not teaching style, or curriculum content, or class management, although all these are featured to some degree. The focus is the individual boy or girl to whom everything is happening. I have tried to look at a small part of the education process as it is experienced by the consumer. It is an impossible task and therefore worth attempting, as a theologian once remarked. With the exception of names and school-uniform colours, every detail and every word spoken is recorded as it occurred. Nothing has been invented.

The resulting data with commentary and questions and more extended information in the form of Sequels at the end of chapters, are intended for students in teacher training and experienced teachers on In-Service activities, as an aid to linking theory with practice.

A problem in teacher training is that participants have rarely all witnessed the same events or taught the same children. An alternative is to discuss film and video. This book will, I hope, offer another possibility, and serve as an introduction to life in the primary school, encouraging all of us to see events from the child's point of view.

Chapter One

Mike, Aged 5

Me dad likes pheasants the best

The School

Mike's junior and infant school has Church of England aided status. The church controls staff appointments, with the local vicar being chairman of the governors. An entry in that intriguing biography of any school, the log book, records the visit in 1890 of the vicar's wife, appropriately named Mrs Crucifix.

In 1970, it was solely a school for the local village, but now its 142 pupils include 24 known as 'itinerants', a term which can include people from canal barges, fairgrounds, circuses, as well as gypsies and tinkers. Those designated 'itinerant' in Mike's school come from a nearby illegal caravan site and their parents are engaged in various casual labouring jobs such as fencing. They are, in fact, second- or third-generation gypsies, rather than true Romanies.

In addition to the headteacher, there are four full-time teachers and one part-timer. Each class is of mixed ability and there is no major reading problem. Nor is there any punishment other than disapproval and over the last thirty years two children only have been caned. For what crimes? one wonders.

The Day

I arrive at the school at 8.50 a.m. on a dull and rainy day near Christmas and the following exchange takes place in the small car park as soon as I get out of my car:

4

Boy (aged about 7):	This is a school, you know.
R. M.:	Is it? How do you know?
Boy:	Well, I'm here. We've been here for a hundred years.
R. M.:	Have you? That's a long time. What's your name?
Boy:	David.

One of the great pleasures of visiting infant and junior schools is that children will often initiate conversations quite unsolicited and tell you it is their birthday, or their mummy has had a baby, or the goldfish has died. It is good for the visitor's ego. Even a monster with one bloodshot eye in the middle of his forehead would find someone holding his hand at play time.

Lorna Ridgway (1976) quotes a headmaster, Mr Ron Waters, as he highlights what are, for him, crucial differences in outlook between young and old. He says:

> When parents and children follow each other into the Head's room, one cannot escape the comparisons. The children are curious, while parents know already; prejudice has replaced their curiosity. Children trust while parents are predominantly fearful and need to be put at ease. Children are spontaneously and intuitively honest in their appreciation of a situation, while parents tend to say what pleases. Lively optimism, curiosity, clear vision and a natural honesty that cuts through cant like a knife, mark the child's approach to life.

It is a view which has echoes of William Blake.

I go into the reception classroom where a few 5-year-olds are playing with toys and building apparatus. The room is fairly small with large windows wholly occupying one side. Christmas decorations are everywhere – a frieze of the Nativity; a Father Christmas cut-out; cotton wool on the windows; a small silver paper tree. There is a nature table area with cress growing and holly (not growing), cones and a log. A carpeted corner of the room serves as a story area and on one of the walls in this part are two newspaper cuttings of two pandas and a notice announcing, SUSAN BROUGHT THESE PICTURES. Occupying another corner of the room is a coat rack with named pegs. Like many modern infant school classrooms, this one has particular sections identified with various activities, so as to combine the best features of organization and accessibility.

5

As any reader of this book will know, it is customary in infant and junior schools for certain parts of the school year to be dominated by festivals which are a part of the Christian and cultural heritage. (A helpful teachers' guide to practical activities at such times is by Brandling, 1978.) Christmas and Easter clearly have considerable impact, both on the curriculum and on the children's consciousness, with related activities often extending over several weeks, and with classwork closely geared to each particular festival, as will be seen throughout these pages.

In such a way, the religious cultural traditions of the society are passed on from generation to generation. As Waller (1932) put it, 'Man and his heirs hold their common property in perpetuum'. Transmission of what has been found valuable in the past, and interchange of new but acceptable ways and ideas, are two sides of the cultural coin.

Moreover, in a culturally diverse context, provision should be made to accommodate a variety of traditions, so as to value both the children's expertise and experience and also the homes from which they come.

Such considerations will, at this point on a Thursday morning, be far from the mind of Mike's teacher, although they may, in a sense, inform what she does.

Mrs Hilton is an experienced teacher in her early 40s, with silvery hair and a pleasant, friendly face. She is very smartly dressed in a purple jumper and tweed skirt. A medallion hangs round her neck. While she is engaged in calling the dinner register, in walks Mike.

Mrs Hilton: Good morning, Mike.
Mike: Good morning.

He is a stocky 5-year-old. He has a chubby face with puffy cheeks and fair curly hair. It is a pleasant, open face with blue eyes and a good complexion. Underneath his thick coat he is wearing a floppy polo-neck sweater and long brown trousers, with a hole in the right knee. Brown boots. Blue socks. He takes off his coat and walks straight into the corner where the children are playing with building materials. He settles down instantly, an indication of the confidence and assurance he is to display throughout the day. 'Learning to live in a classroom', as Philip

Jackson (1968) observes, 'involves, among other things, learning
to live in a crowd.'
  By 9.10 a.m. the attendance and dinner registers have been
called and the twenty-three children, nine of whom are designated
'itinerant', move to the story corner. Such consistent localizing of
specific activities helps to develop a sense of security and order
in young children. It also serves to heighten the ritualistic power
of an occasion and, as we shall see throughout this book, ritual
plays a powerful part in school life.
  Mike has put his ruler in his trousers as a sword. He now
takes a glove puppet but is skilfully and surreptitiously relieved
of this by Mrs Hilton. It is done so quietly that no one realizes it
has happened. In such a way do sensitive teachers, and parents,
avoid conflict where possible, and it is by no means as easy to
put into practice as it may seem to the casual observer.
  All the children are now sitting down on the floor, except Mike
who walks about in an alert but nonchalant supervisory manner.
Mrs Hilton begins the Nativity story with a short homily on the
condition of the picture book she has in her hand. Notice the
simple but effective narrative setting she adopts at the start, with
quoted conversation between herself and Miss Barling. It makes
the moral more immediate for her listeners, and virtually turns
the torn book into an injured party.

Mrs H.:   Well, yesterday afternoon, when you'd all gone home,
          will you listen please, Billy, Miss Barling came in the
          classroom and she very kindly said, 'Shall I put the
          book corner tidy?' So I said, 'Oh, yes please, because
          I've got so much to clear up'.
Mike: Today.
Mrs H.:   Last night this was. So she made the book corner
          all nice and tidy and she found this lovely book for
          us. It's sad because some of the book has been torn,
          yes I'll tell you about this in a minute, sit down, I'll
          show you. I don't think it was you children because
          I haven't mended this book and somebody has. So I
          don't think it was anyone in this class. It's rather sad,
          isn't it, because a lovely book like that (*Mike explains
          that another teacher had already told them that story,
          and Mrs Hilton, not at all put out, says*) Did she?
Mike: Yeah.

Mrs H.: Well, I thought I'd read a little bit of it, because it's getting very near to Christmas and, do you know what it says there? (*pointing to the title on the cover*).
Child: Bethlehem.
Mrs H.: No.
Mike: Angel.
Mrs H.: No.
Child: Angels come from Bethlehem, don't they?
Mrs H.: Erm. Well, they went *to* Bethlehem, to tell the shepherd about Jesus.
Child: Fairies.
Mrs H.: No. It says, 'The Christmas Book'. 'The Christmas Book'. And the first part of the story, I'm sorry Natalie, isn't there, but that means you know the first part of the story don't you?
Children: Yes.
Mrs H.: Where did Mary and Joseph live?
Mike: In a shed. That shed there. (*He points to a picture on the wall.*)
Mrs H.: But where did they live before they went there, Mike?
Child: Bethlehem.
Mrs H.: No.
Child: In a cottage.
Mrs H.: Well, I suppose you could call it a little cottage. It wasn't like the little cottage you know. A little house in (*pause*) NAZARETH. Can you say it?
Children: Nazareth.
Mrs H.: And what did Joseph do?
Child: Carpenter.
Mrs H.: He was a ...
Children: Carpenter.
Mrs H.: And what is a carpenter?
Mike: What makes carps.
Mrs H.: No, he doesn't make carps. He makes things ...
Child: Wood.
Mrs H.: Out of wood. Good boy. Don't shout.
Child: And he makes some chairs.
Mrs H.: He makes chairs and ...
Mike: Tables.
Mrs H.: Tables and ...
Child: Bookcases ... book

8

Mrs H.:	Well, (*unintelligible*) ... wouldn't use today.
Child:	And and and he would and he would make a new book like this.
Mrs H.:	I shouldn't think so. He would make chairs like that ... Michele and Matthew and Sean are sitting on, wouldn't he, because that's made of wood.
Child:	And cardboard.
Mrs H.:	Are they? (*Several children talk at once.*) A wooden bench and tables. Very good, Warren. Well done. All right. And then they had to go on a long journey (*interruptions by several children*) ... to Bethlehem. And how did they get to Bethlehem?
Child:	On a donkey.
Mrs H.:	Well, Mary was on a donkey.
Child:	(*shouting*) And Joseph walked.
Child:	And Joseph walked a long way.
Mrs H.:	He walked a long, long way, and they were ...
Mike:	And they were so tired.
Child:	And they stopped.
Mrs H.:	So tired.
Child:	And they stopped in a lay-by.
Mrs H.:	They stopped in in a lay-by? Oh, I don't think (*laughing*) they had lay-bys in those days, not like we have. They would stop on the side of the road. Yes, I suppose it was a lay-by really, wasn't it?

And so on. Mrs Hilton has superb, quiet control. She employs a considerable voice range, with a heightening of intonation and stress, almost automatic for talking with very young children. Perhaps dangerously so. Joyce Grenfell's splendid parody about Sidney and Co. reminds us of the thin dividing line between an intonation and manner which is accommodating and warm, and one which is patronizing. It is a tight-rope which every infants teacher treads and, in an oblique way, calls to mind a curiously symbolic and oddly disturbing story told by John Holt (1974). A lady, shopping in a crowded New York department store, saw, walking in front of her, two charming small boys. Feeling affectionate, she patted them on the top of their heads, only to discover, when they turned round and looked up at her, that they were rather angry midgets. Presumably, in common with certain other minority groups, they could cope with such intrusions on their privacy and personality. Young children must often endure being addressed as if they were budgerigars, puppies, deaf, or senile.

But Mrs Hilton makes no such errors. She involves the children in the story, by using familiar language and constructions; by asking questions and then allowing time for reply; by showing pictures; by praising correct answers and by salvaging what she can from wrong responses; by laughing at errors; by displaying good humour. It is generally the kind of approach which the psychologist B. F. Skinner might endorse, as consistent with his theory of rewarding positive responses, thereby encouraging repetition of them.

Above all, Mrs Hilton has a high level of rapport with the children as she relates, where she can, the story world to their experience. At one point, a little later, she says: 'Do you know, when I got home from the concert last night, there was a telephone message for me to say that my cousin had had a little baby boy, but he wasn't born in a stable.'

Mike: Where was he born?
Mrs H.: He was born in a hospital. That's nowadays, that's prob-
         ably where we shall find babies being born. Certainly
         not in a stable.
Child: I was born in a hospital.

The children, who are, of course, familiar with the story, respond to the teacher's prompting with enthusiasm and energy. Mike, meanwhile, has picked up a copy of Grimm's fairy tales and is now sitting above all the others on a cupboard, turning over the pages of this book, but missing nothing of the Christmas story or the pictures in the teacher's book. He looks at the picture of the three wise men and exclaims:

Mike: Black man! Bat man! That black one was in the middle
         and now he's in the front.
Mrs H.: Oh, yes. Well, they must have altered that. Yes, you're
         right, Mike. Well done!

The story continues and Mrs Hilton takes the opportunity, where it easily presents itself, as it did in the tale of the torn book, of developing or reinforcing the children's sense of morality. At one point a child says:

Child:	I got some ... I ... I ... I stole some treasure ... two treasures.
Mrs H.:	You stole some treasure? That's not very good, is it? You don't steal things.
Child:	You mustn't steal money from the bank.
Mrs H.:	You mustn't steal money from anywhere.
Child:	That's bank robbers. That's bank robbers.
Children:	(*General hubbub*) ... robber ... bank ... terrible ... bank ... I'm in the bank.

For a short while the Christmas story has to compete with the rival claims of bank robbers. It's touch and go for a moment, but the 2,000-year-old narrative reasserts itself (or the teacher has her own way). The story comes to an end. The picture book is put back on the shelf and Mrs Hilton says, 'Shall we sing "Away in a Manger?"'

Mike:	No.
Children:	Yes.
Mrs H.:	Not now, dear. Sit up. (*Various children's voices.*) Yes, I know. Oh, just a minute, please. Let's wait for Mike, shall we ... (*unintelligible*) ... Well, yes, he knew where I wanted to put it, actually. Thank you, Mike. That ... Stand it up, that's it. Good boy. Come on, then. Dear, oh, dear. Come on, Andrew, sit down. Right. Stephen, will you ... Ready ...

Children and Mrs H. (*singing*):
> Away in a manger, no crib for a bed,
> The little Lord Jesus laid down his sweet head.
> The stars in the bright sky looked down where he lay,
> The little Lord Jesus asleep on the hay.

Mike:	(*running his finger up and down the page*) Up and down up and down up and down.

Children and Mrs H. (*singing*):
> The cattle are lowing, the baby awakes,
> But little Lord Jesus no crying he makes.
> I love thee, Lord Jesus, look down from the sky,

	And stay by my bedside till morning is nigh.
Mike:	Up and down up and down up and down.
Mrs H.:	(*to a child*) You don't know 'The Cattle Shed'? Well, you shall sing it, you shall sing it. Put your hands together. Close your eyes. Thank you, dear God, for sending
Mike:	Thank you, dear God
Mrs H.:	Shall we just listen, Mike please.
	Thank you, dear God, for sending baby Jesus to us at Christmas time. Help us to think of all babies and be kind to them.
Children:	And be kind to them.
Mrs H.:	Bless mummies and daddies and sisters and brothers and all the others in God's great family.
All:	Amen.

After this prayer, which will be echoed at the end of the day, there are two more short carols.

It is plain that Mike is a dominant character. He has already shown several instances of initiative and leadership and is to show many more as the day proceeds. I doubt if he has missed one word that has been spoken. He has finished sentences begun by Mrs Hilton; interjected comments; asked questions; answered many, both right and wrong; made suggestions; been quick to do classroom jobs, such as making visible on top of the blackboard the picture book which Andrew had wrongly placed.

As an extrovert, divergent, independent person, he could on so many occasions, have been squashed by his teacher. Constantly in conflict and nagged *ad nauseam*. Instead, his energies are skilfully channelled and put to good use with an art which conceals the art. His antics with another teacher later this afternoon will highlight the expert handling he is receiving now from Mrs Hilton. To one teacher he is a lively and likeable leader; to the other, a pest.

King (1977) comments on the indirect techniques of social control used by infant teachers. His description monitors Mrs Hilton in an uncanny way.

Little shaming and blaming are used. The verbal methods used instead include the no-need-to-answer-question, e.g. 'Are you getting on with your work?', said to someone obviously not doing so, and complete the sentence, e.g. 'And when we've finished our paintings we must?' ... pupils chorus, 'wash our hands.' Children quickly learn the nuances of meanings in the teacher's voice. These include the 'now we are going to do something exciting' voice, the 'slightly, aggrieved sad' voice, and the 'I am being very patient with you' voice (examples, perhaps, of restricted codes). Infant teachers also show professional equanimity, they are not upset when someone wets the floor; and professional affection, shown in their smiling faces and physical contact with children, holding hands and lap sitting, and in their use of endearments.

Only half an hour has yet gone by, and many of these features have been seen.

At 9.30 a.m. the children move to various tables for different activities. Andrew tries valiantly to approach a seat from under the table. As he comes up, rather like a bemused pot-holer, Mike, ever vigilant, squashes his face with his hand. It has the window pane effect of flattened nose and crumpled lips as he says, 'No. No. This is Billy's seat', and so it turns out to be.

There are three tables, each with about seven children. One group is finishing parental Christmas presents. Another is involved in a brick-building exercise whereby they fit together five small blocks, draw the shape on a piece of paper and write down the number of blocks.

The children in this group are now involved in a matching exercise designed to encourage the skills of one-to-one correspondence; visual discrimination; sorting into sets; colour differentiation, and to develop some awareness of key terms, such as *more, less, greater, as many as, how many*. Plastic objects such as pigs, dogs, spanners, Land Rovers, are to be sorted according to colour or kind into a plastic tray, divided up into different compartments for the purpose. Mike settles down quickly to the work, making car noises as he plays with one of the racing cars, while sorting his objects into identical pairs. At one point, Peter addresses Wayne as 'You bloody pitch'. With a change of 'p' for 'b', it could reflect his father's language.

Until now, the children have completely ignored my presence, either in the classroom or in this group. Having had a student teacher for the previous six weeks, they are apparently used to relative strangers. In any event, their own activities are much more interesting and engaging. And it allows me to record their activities more or less uninterrupted.

13

Led by Andrew, ('itinerant' in fact as well as designation having, at the age of 5, already attended schools in Scotland, Wales and Lincolnshire), four of the children in this group now decide to use their little plastic objects to play Cowboys and Indians. The green horsemen are lined up in battle formation and the children shoot each other with gun-shaped fists and fingers. Mrs Hilton works, for the moment, with the gift-making group, then, aware of these diversions, comes over to convert the children away from Cowboys and Indians and back to the matching task. Such rapid change of focus of attention by teachers will be familiar to all with experience. Philip Jackson (1968) found in one study of primary school classrooms that 'the teacher engages in as many as a thousand interpersonal interchanges each day'. Such an integral part of the job presupposes flexibility and sensitivity.

Mrs Hilton returns to her former table and, within a minute, battle formations again take precedence. Wayne says to Mike, 'Eh! you can have that spear for stabbing', and gives him a little plastic hand-saw, which Mike, entirely absorbed, accepts. Andrew and Billy start snatching each other's objects and off goes Mike, previously protective, you will remember, of Billy's territory, round the table to wreak vengeance on Andrew, chanting: 'Here comes a bomber ... Here's the Long [*sic*] Ranger ... '

There is, momentarily, absolute silence in the room, such as is thought by some to denote an angel's presence, as Tracy comes through the door, one hour late for school. Michele is sent to the headteacher with the revised dinner numbers. Twenty plus three.

Billy and Mike now have a friendly fight, which stops suddenly after two or three seconds, when Mike observes, 'Eh! Tracy's come' (two minutes after her actual arrival). Billy and Mike are instantly the best of pals again. Mike picks up a folded card marked PEAS, says, 'This is an Indian's tent', and tosses it at Jonty who passively accepts it.

There is a compulsive quality about these plastic objects. The games vary from Matching, to Cowboys and Indians, to Bombing Each Other, and the objects are excellent vehicles for the children's imaginations. Duller objects might be preferred, on the grounds that the teacher-initiated activity would then stand more of a chance, but I think this would be proved false. At this stage in their development fantasy is more powerful than reality. The children are using real objects as symbols, endowing them with several attributes, and this would seem to indicate the pre-operational thought stage identified by Piaget. The children are handling small pieces, manipulating them into different relationships. When they have had adequate physical experience of this kind, they will, without immediately losing their interest in such activity, become more able to manipulate symbol and thought, where previously they could only deal in objects. The very process of reading involves such a transition, from the object to the word, which is a symbol, a conjuring up, of that object in the mind's eye.

The value and potential of the kind of play which leads to educational development is well summarized by Parry and Archer (1975):

Play enables the child to test his competence in many ways without fear of failure, and this in turn builds up his concept of self and self-esteem. He faces problems in play and learns how to overcome them, since play provides an outlet for his strong feelings. He learns about his relationships with other children through sharing experiences with them, making friends, and observing how other children behave. He suffers experiences connected with being a boy or a girl, a leader or a follower, older or younger, stronger or weaker. Play encourages a child to use language, by providing a variety of first-hand experiences which stimulate him to develop skills which are necessary to cope with the complex world in which he is growing up.

At 9.55 a.m. Mike takes his tray off to Mrs Hilton who says, 'Good boy, Mike. That's splendid. There are one or two more down there'. He returns to the table and, within half a minute, he and Billy have a fight, actually punching each other. Mike says, 'I'm not going to play with you when we go out. I'm going to play with Wayne.' The teacher speaks patiently to the fighters and they calm down.

The apparently anti-social behaviour which has occurred so far – fighting, squabbling, pushing, bombing no less – may appear more serious when recorded in print than it seemed at the time. Perhaps these young children do not have the language to negotiate personal transactions and need to resort to physical contact which, within the context of this reception class, does not seem particularly inappropriate. Certainly, Mrs Hilton appears often to act on the behaviourist assumption that many of the misdemeanours may be ignored and they will die

15

away, given time and the right atmosphere. Like Argos, she is well aware of everything that is happening in the room, but chooses her encounters selectively, rarely rebuking directly, for that would highlight the fault. Instead she diverts combatants into more acceptable forms of behaviour, by turning their attention to their tasks.

She now comes to join our group and asks Mike to show her two cars. This he does.

Mrs H.: Billy, will you show me three little pigs?
     (Billy, hesitantly, counts three pigs into her hand.)
Mrs H.: Peter, you give me four little dogs.

Mike interrupts and counts six dogs into her hand, some blue, some red. The fact that he refers to one of them as yellow suggests that his understanding of colours is not yet clearly established. Although intelligent enough, he may have missed out on some kinds of pre-school experiences.

Wayne counts out five house into Mrs Hilton's hand. Andrew is asked for three cars. He gives four, then takes one away. Jonty is asked to give two racing cars to Matthew; she gives him four. Matthew is asked for five little lambs. And so on, with each child getting a turn, not only at developing counting and discriminatory skills, but also at working with an adult and with other children, thereby developing those social skills of accommodation and co-operation, of give and take (literally), which, it is hoped, will eventually minimize unacceptable behaviour.

The children obviously need to put a finger on each of the objects and not take their eyes off it. Memory and recall cannot serve for physical and visual contact, and there appears to be a security in touching. At such a transitional, pre-operational stage as this their answers are characterized by inconsistency. They are sometimes right and sometimes wrong. They appear to have, as yet, no firm grasp of number concept.

For a short while now Mrs Hilton varies the routine with a different kind of activity: 'How many boats have I got? She holds up two boats ... five race horses ... and so on. Each time, Mike is the first to answer, thereby indicating not only his relative alertness, but also one of the inherent difficulties of asking questions of a whole group. It is the weak who need the practice.

16

All the children are now asked to clear away their materials. This is another aspect of their socialization and of the classroom ritual. It helps familiarize the children with their own immediate environment and it gives them a sense of responsibility in caring for materials and tools. Once again one is reminded of Mrs Hilton's unfailing courtesy towards the children, by the manner in which she requests Andrew to get a tissue for his runny nose.

For a few seconds Mike lies under his chair, flat out, counting blobs of white plastic on the floor. Then he joins the rest of the children in clearing up and walks in triumph, like a proud butler, carrying seven white plastic trays to where they are stored. A little girl stops him en route and says, 'You're my friend, aren't you?' but the overture is rejected with a shake of the head. He is the last to finish and the teacher, instead of rebuking him, says, 'How are you getting on? Have you nearly finished down there, Mike?'

Most of the other children are now in the story corner. They sing a finger rhyme and then talk about the weather. Mike has permission to go to the toilet. The children are asked what weather it is and Helen says, 'It's snowing. No, raining'. In fact, it is neither. She finds the card which announces IT IS CLOUDY, which it is.

Mike's excursion has taken one minute. He returns and Andrew is allowed to go to the toilet. Andrew returns shortly and another child sets off. A kind of chain reaction. Mrs Hilton knows that toilet visiting, like confession, is best accomplished singly.

All the children are now sitting down in the corner but Mike is the only one with a book ('Ladybird'). It is news time and they are talking about what has happened to them. Such autobiographical news sessions are common in primary schools, but diminish as children grow older. They give an ideal opportunity for the children to relate the worlds of home and school and for them to use language in a natural and realistic context in that they are speaking of concerns and interests close to their hearts. Above all, perhaps, the message is implicit that the children's own interests have significance and importance. They have a validity at this stage which, somehow, seems to be rarely fully realized in secondary school.

Tracy is about to tell us of her lion hunt. Can that really be the reason for her lateness this morning? We shall never know, for she fails to say anything. Mrs Hilton exhorts her to think about it tonight and tell us tomorrow.

Mrs H.: Has anyone else got anything to tell us?
Sean.: Barry gave me a new car.

This comment is missed by most in the general hubbub, but Mike, apparently absorbed in his book, has heard it and repeats it.

Mrs H.: Katy, what have you got to tell us? (*No response.*)
Child: I've got a goldfish and it's name is Deborah.
Stephen: Daddy's got a car and it's orange, red and yellow.

The teacher accepts what each child has to offer and repeats each response, thereby reinforcing it and establishing it as a piece of knowledge to be mediated to the others. Jonty is now sitting on her lap as she continues to ask the children, 'What have you got to tell us? If a child cannot answer there is a slight chorus from three or four braver spirits: 'He's too shy, too shy.'

Helen: My mummy says one has to sleep at one end and one has to sleep at the other end.
Mike: My brother sleeps down the same end as my end and my sister sleeps down the other end.
Mrs H.: How many live in your trailer?
Mike: Five. There's me mum, and she's called 'Mummy'. And there's me dad. He's called 'Uncle Mike' and he specially likes eating pheasants. My dad eats them swans and when they got them long necks he eats everything off it.

Teachers are, inevitably, recipients of much personal information, sometimes mundane and dull; sometimes bizarre and contradictory; sometimes confidential and even embarrassing. The role, which may in secondary school be that of sympathetic counsellor, or dispenser of justice, is here that of gentle interviewer or facilitator.

Matthew, who, meanwhile, has been playing with a mechanical toy, is asked to show it to the rest of the children 'Then he won't need to play with it all the time, will he children?' It is a crafty, professional ploy for capitalizing on his inattention. Further evidence, if it were now needed, of Mrs Hilton's excellent management techniques. Matthew winds up the car and off it goes, much to everyone's enjoyment. We next see Katy's mechanical mouse, which chases its own tail, and then the children briefly discuss the difference between mice and squirrels. Every incident is an occasion for language.

At 10.35 a.m. the bell sounds for break and the children put on their coats. Mike tries to claim sanctuary in the classroom on account of a cold, but is informed, 'The fresh air will do you good'. A euphemism for 'out you go', but more positive. He duly goes out with the others and Mrs Hilton and I have coffee and cake (a colleague's birthday) in the staff room.

While some schools vary breaktimes according to their activities, or even allow children to choose their own relaxation periods, most primary schools order their day along fairly similar lines. A common pattern, as indicated by Hilsum and Cane (1971), is as follows:

School starts	A.M. Break begins	A.M Break ends	Morning School ends	Afternoon School begins	P.M. Break begins	P.M. Break ends	School finishes
8.55	10.40	10.55	12.00	1.30	2.30	2.40	3.30

It is a pattern which has stood the test of time and as readily adopts to a National Curriculum as to earlier structures.

At 11.00 a.m. we return to the classroom, where the children are hanging up their coats, before moving to the school hall for singing around the piano. Initially they sit on the floor, but, when Mike elects to sit on a chair, four others follow suit. The hall is narrow, small and cold. There are some climbing frames at the side, a Christmas frieze around the walls, and a stage prepared for a concert (which occurred the night before).

The children sing the song 'Say Little Squirrel', an appropriate choice in view of the earlier comparison between mice and squirrels. Questions are asked on the narrative of the song, with Mike, as earlier, foremost in answering. In this kind of context, comprehension becomes a natural and sensible activity. When the children repeat the song, Mike takes off his shoe and inspects his sock. Then a new song for them to learn:

> Here is a snowman, big and white.
> Isn't he a funny sight?
> Let's make a snowball,
> Toss it at his hat.
> Off it goes,
> Just like that.

Mike elects to clap in time to the music and says, 'I was clapping at the end'. He was, in fact, the only child to do so and, for most of the songs that followed, he adopted his own individual routine. Music is that kind of liberating medium for adults, as for children; it permits an imaginative response in terms of physical movement of some kind. Some current research indicates that music will even provoke movement from a foetus in the womb. How much more so from young children, although none of the others reacted quite in Mike's individual manner, except in imitation of him. During 'Yankee Doodle Dandy' (the most popular song, along with 'Jingle Bells') he danced in time to the music. One other child followed his lead. During the singing of 'Mary Had a Little Lamb' he mimed playing a guitar and was imitated by two others.

However, these activities did not dull his other responses. For example, when the children had sung

> Merrily, merrily over the snow,
> Merrily, merrily sleighing we go,

they were asked the meaning of 'sleighing'. Mike was the first to answer and replied. 'Ski-ing over the snow'. During another song he led the matching of finger counting with the appropriate line:

> Five little jingle bells fell in the snow.
> Four little jingle bells fell in the snow.
> Three little jingle bells fell in the snow.
> Two little jingle bells fell in the snow.
> One little jingle bell fell in the snow.

What such a song may lack in drama and excitement, it makes up for in security and familiarity perhaps.

The songs, seven of them in all, were punctuated by instructions to the children with regard to sitting down, singing louder and so on, all done in a very gentle, courteous but firm tone. The children were reasonably attentive for the most part, with the exception of Eddie, who spent his time and energy in trying to squeeze himself between wall and piano, an activity he accomplished quite successfully.

The music lesson finishes at 11.30 a.m., by which time the children have, unknowingly, had experience of oral comprehension and language development, of rhythm and rhyme, of exercise of memory. In addition to any intrinsic attraction, all these are useful pre-reading activities. They have also been involved in an interesting and enjoyable corporate activity, as well as exercising specific musical accomplishments.

Mrs Hilton now gives instructions for the next session. The red group will first go to the toilet and then back to the classroom for a puzzle. The yellow table will follow this sequence, but they should have their reading books ready. Very young children seldom find it easy to retain a future set of events in their heads, or plan in advance on the basis of verbal instructions. According to Piaget, it will not be until the stage of 'concrete operations' (that is, around 7 to 11 years) is reached that, with the establishment of the sequencing of events, concepts about time will be clarified. These children have as yet a very hazy notion of time, and need constant practise, of the kind that the teacher is here giving, at anticipating events. Constant explanations and predictions of future sequences of activity are, perhaps, not too common in infant schools. It is language experience which may be unwittingly neglected.

We are now back in the classroom for the last session of the morning, which is related to pre-reading and pre-writing work.

The children on one table are given papers with patterns which they have to continue. Such work will, it is hoped, develop left to right eye co-ordination; awareness of shapes; visual discrimination; sequencing.

A second group is required to crayon a coloured line, following the arrows on the paper.

A third group is with the teacher responding to flash cards using words from the 'Happy Venture' reading scheme by Fred Schonell (Edinburgh: Oliver & Boyd). When news comes that some of the boys are playing in the toilets, that natural mecca for the more sociable in any school, Mrs Hilton sets off in missionary style to reclaim the lost, and soon returns with Mike and Billy, both of whom come skipping in.

Mike joins the flash card group and the teacher continues the activity of holding up cards with single words on them for the children to recognize. At this stage, it is a testing, rather than teaching, exercise.

here   (no takers)

fluff   (recognized by some children)

Dick   (Mike says 'Jane')

Nip   (Mike says 'ball')

Each time the children are wrong, Mrs Hilton laughs and says, 'No it isn't. What does it say?' Natalie, who has arrived from another group armed with her own reading book, despairs of such amateur guesswork and proceeds to point out to her peers the characters in the story.

The sentence on card, 'Here is Dick', is held up. 'Which word says *here?*' asks the teacher. Mike points to *is*. For all his alertness and intelligence, he has not yet got to grips with reading, although that is not surprising at this early stage. However, he does have the confidence to guess and, provided that can eventually be channelled so as to become less haphazard and unthinking, it will stand him in good stead.

Mrs Hilton determines on another strategy. Mike and the rest of the group are now each given cards with their first name on, a hardboard square, and a St Bruno tobacco tin containing a large lump of Plasticine. If the flash-card letters are too small for some, then they may benefit from making larger letters themselves with the Plasticine and seeing, perhaps, something of how the shapes are made up. At the same time, they will be engaged in something almost magical – a kind of creation of themselves out of an indistinguishable lump. Since Wayne is about to copy his name upside down, acting against my intention of trying to remain completely uninvolved, I turn his card the right way up, eliciting a look of utter amazement.

Billy says, 'I can't do my name', and Mike comments, 'Baby, baby, baby'. They elbow each other, smiling the while, and, after a few prods, return to the Plasticine task, which grips them as they grip it.

Meanwhile, the arrow continuation and shape duplication groups carry on with their work, and all the children are actively absorbed for a quarter of an hour, a long time for 5-year-olds. During this time, the teacher has been constantly on the go – giving instructions and advice to individuals; focusing attention on the task in hand; moving from group to group and child to child, with the concern of an Olympics coach.[1] She remains courteous and pleasant, without being sentimental; firm and clear-headed, without bullying or nagging.

At 12.01 p.m., junior school prefects arrive heralding news of dinner and, with such an incentive, the children clear their desks remarkably quickly. 120 children stay for school dinner and, such is the limitation of space, that classrooms and corridors have to be used, despite the intense cold. Over the decades, many schools have grown accustomed to tolerating unacceptable conditions.

While the preparations were being made, I talked with Mike for a few minutes, recording the conversation on tape. Billy was with us in the staff room, as moral support for Mike. It was strange that such an apparently extrovert and confident boy as Mike should have needed a companion, but he certainly was not going to talk without one.

The purpose of the chat was to learn a little of Mike's home and family, and it emerged that he lived in a white trailer, which he preferred to a house, with brother Peter, sister Chérie, mother (Aunt Jean) and father (Uncle Mike). In answer to my question about what he had done in school during the morning, he told me of a fight he had had some time earlier in which he and Billy and Eddie were matched against 'the big boys ... the very big boys', and everyone won. Such information was obviously of much greater significance than anything that had happened in the classroom, and the only thing that he could or would recall from the morning was that Tracy had come in late. It is strange how odd incidents remain in the mind.

Telling me that his favourite dinner was jam on toast, we ended our somewhat bizarre conversation with an exchange about the preferences of his dad.

Mike: Me dad likes pheasants the best.
R. M.: Yes, I heard you say your dad likes pheasants (*i.e. earlier in the morning in class*). Does he catch them himself?
Mike: No. He kills them with these wheels.
R. M.: How does he do it? How does he kill them?

---

1 A completely different approach to the teaching of reading is offered by Liz Waterland (1985).

Mike: Look. Look. He don't bib his horn. You just go ... He just, he just let his motors run at them at them ... when it's very far he goes brrrrrh!

R. M.: And that kills the pheasants?

Mike: Yeah. He killed two this, four that time with one ... one wheel ... two went on his back wheels, two went on his front wheels.

R. M.: Dear. Four pheasants.

This is a subject near to Mike's heart and he talks with enthusiasm and energy, describing the pheasants' manner of Boadicea-type death quite graphically. Language which closely involves the speaker is almost invariably richer, more vivid and more interesting. It also reveals more of the self.

After ten minutes' conversation, we are back at 12.15 p.m. in the classroom, where the tables have been laid for dinner. One teacher is using the waiting time in hearing a child read. Another teacher is doing finger rhyme songs with the rest of the children, 'hands and fingers/knees and toes ... '

At 12.20 p.m. we all sit down to mashed potatoes, sausages, beans, bacon; followed by apple pie and custard. I am sitting with Sean, Tracy, Katie, Peter, Stephen, Mike, Billy, and we chat about school and home, food and television, before getting caught up in a 'Can you do this?' sequence, i.e. we offer to each other for imitation ever more complex finger contortions.

After dinner the children play outside in the asphalt play-ground and I talk with the headteacher who, like many in schools, constantly has his break interrupted for a thousand and one reasons.

At 1.25 p.m. the class reassembles and, for a few minutes, most of the children play with toys and are supervised by the ancillary dinner lady. It is useful settling-in period for the children to become adjusted once again to the classroom via the security of familiar and loved objects such as toys, as well as being part of their social education.

The class is to be taken for the first part of the afternoon by another teacher, Mrs Champion, an elderly, silver-haired, rather stately person. The children are ready, grouped in the story corner, when Billy's father arrives to take him off to his grandmother's, some 120 miles away in Doncaster. It is a sudden, and perhaps permanent, move. So he misses the tale of Rodney, the hamster, who eats a good deal and likes wandering about the kitchen. This is an appropriate post-prandial story in which the children are absolutely absorbed, as they often are by fantasy about pet animals.

The food motif is continued in the poem of Mary Jane and her rice pudding by A. A. Milne. It is recited solely by Mrs Champion, who is concerned to promote skills of clear diction and elocution.

It is difficult to say how appropriate such verse is, for children like the strangest things. It has rhythm and structure, and allows scope for a reasonable intonation range. But, apart from the weakness of at least two of the rhymes, its chief problem seems to be that it echoes a middle-class, early-twentieth-century world, remote from this one. Its language and context are foreign to Mike and his peers. Moreover, it does not say very much of interest.

Furthermore, reception-age children do not listen easily unless they are physically involved in some way. So, from poetry to mime, and the children stand around the teacher holding up imaginary dandelion flowers, which they blow when appropriate for the words.

> One o'clock, two o'clock, three o'clock, four;
> I've got a fairy clock close to my door.
> Five o'clock, six o'clock, seven o'clock, eight;
> I blew and I blew and I found it was late.
> I blew and I blew till I counted to ten,
> And now I begin all over again.

The rhyme ends and the children have almost blown themselves into extinction, such is the enthusiasm of willing participants, who practically need to be protected from themselves. In fact, they are becoming rather restless and noisy, and the tape recording of the next poem is only partially audible. The problem is, again, their lack of involvement in what is a monologue, recited without pictures, and with physical actions related only tenuously to a difficult text. The poem, 'The King's Breakfast', is again by A. A. Milne, and both may be found in his volume, *When We Were Very Young*, published by Methuen. The mistaken substitution at one point by Mrs Champion of 'Dairymaid' for 'Alderney' only exacerbates language problems which are taxing enough anyway.

Mike, all this while, has been following the teacher with his eyes and performing such actions as there were with his hands, but he does not know the words. It is a similar pattern to that he adopted during the morning's music in the hall.

He is given permission to go to the toilet and, on return, decides to seek his own amusement among the coats hanging on their pegs. While the other children are involved in a variety of poems and mimes – banging imaginary cymbals on the march; hammering 'bing, bang, bong' on the floor; reaching up into the air and down to the ground, as Teddy bears; walking about chanting 'tick, tock, tick, tock' – Mike is hiding away behind the cupboard, moving in and out of the coats, lying on the floor beside a box.

Three or four other boys follow his lead, forming an energetic if, as yet, rather cautious splinter group. Observing this withdrawal, or diversion, of labour, Mrs Champion remains very patient throughout, occasionally retrieving one of the recalcitrants, only to lose another. Her class is disintegrating and she adopts the efficacious tactic of dramatising 'Twelve Currant Buns in a Baker's Shop'. Under the guise of seeking *more currant buns*, i.e. children to take parts in the narrative about to unfold, she manages to retrieve most of them. The promise of physical involvement wins over all but the hard core of coat dodgers and the song begins.

> Twelve currant buns in a baker's shop,
> Nice and round with sugar on the top.
> A boy came in, with a penny one day,
> Bought a currant bun and took it away.

A child, alias a currant bun, is led away beaming with pleasure, and the song runs its inexorable course for twelve verses, much to the delight of all but the two or three deviants. One of these is Mike, and another, four and a half-year-old Peter. This boy had been very quiet all morning, but became quite lively during the coat campaign, enjoying himself, finding his feet, and getting acclimatized. It is a credit point to salvage from the afternoon session so far. Some of the children would obviously enjoy, and benefit from, a large play area where they could hide – a play house or its equivalent.

Towards 2.20p.m., the children are becoming particularly buoyant and the titles of the last two songs assume an ironic

26

significance: 'Where Are You? Where Are You?' and 'I Hear Thunder. I Hear Thunder'. However, ten minutes later, having donned cardigans, jumpers and anoraks, they are out in the playground, where they need to be.

The benefit of such a break is clear at 2.45 p.m., when the children reassemble with Mrs Hilton for the last session of their day. They are spoken to courteously but firmly and, duly chastened (such news and noise travels fast), sit in the story corner to await further developments.

A similar sequence of activities to that before break now begins, with the exception that all the children act, sing, mime, move, as a group, fully integrated into the activity. They are the same children, but not the same, such is the effect of teacher on pupils and the interaction between them. There are no coat dodgers now, no noisy wanderers, as they all go through their paces and sing 'The Farmer's in His Den'; 'Fair Rosie was a Lovely Girl', 'Here We Go Luby Loo'. Mike plays a major role now in these dramatizations, galloping around the circle as a prince; weaving in and out as an elephant; giving Stephen a kiss. When a messenger comes in for a brush and pan, Mike darts off to get it for her. 'Thank you, Mike. That was very sensible', says Mrs Hilton.

Then, at 3.15 p.m., came one of those golden moments in an infants' classroom, when any unoccupied adult who is present might meditate for a moment on lost innocence and the transience of human life. All the children were standing in the middle of the floor, with their hands together and their eyes closed, as they sang with their teacher the home-time prayer:

> Jesus taught
> That his children ought
> To forgive one another each day,
> And to give and take
> For his dear sake,
> So help us all we pray.
> And it's rough and tumble,
> Rattle and noise;
> Mothers and fathers,
> Girls and boys;
> Baby in the carry cot,
> Cat by the stove;
> A little bit of quarrelling,
> A lot of love.

Thus, the afternoon is rounded off as an occasion, with ritual and order, and a reinforcement of Christianity and morality, the last two lines of the prayer serving as an appropriate summary of what has happened this December day.

At 3.18 p.m., the bell rings and, one by one, the children either go out to find their parents or wait in the classroom to be collected. It is a natural, regular and valuable contact between parents and teachers. One parent asks about a reading book for her child. Another comes to complain. He tells Mrs Hilton that she has gone over time; that time is money to him; and that she should release his son immediately on the bell. Mrs Hilton is as courteous with this man as with her infants and explains about the danger of running straight outside into the road. The father is unimpressed and clearly appreciates nothing of the the problems of buttoning coats, tying shoes, zipping up anoraks.

After a day with 5-year-olds, the adult world has reasserted itself.

Sequel 1 Religious Education

The Education Act 1944

RELIGIOUS EDUCATION IN COUNTY AND VOLUNTARY SCHOOLS

25(2) Subject to the provisions of this section, religious instruction shall be given in every county school and in every voluntary school.

Education Reform Bill

PRINCIPAL PROVISIONS

6(1) In relation to any maintained school and any school year, it shall be the duty of the local education authority and the governing body to exercise their functions with a view to securing, and the duty of the headteacher to secure:

(1) that the National Curriculum as subsisting at the beginning of that year is implemented;
(2) that section 5 of this Act is not contravened; and
(3) that section 25(2) of the 1944 Act (compulsory religious instruction) is complied with.

Many of the formal and informal exchanges between members of Mrs Hilton's class reflect both the legal requirements and educational judgements currently operative in England about the necessity and validity of religious education in schools.

Clearly, as this is an account of one December day in the life of a reception class in a Church of England primary school, the explicitly religious stories, songs and other activities focus on the Christian celebration of Christmas. However, apart from the particularities of the teacher's treatment of this festival on this occasion, the situation as described highlights many of the larger questions and issues surrounding the purposes, aims and methods of teaching R.E. in schools.

These questions and issues become highly significant when it is realized that British schools are set in a society which is recognizably and unashamedly, pluralist. The principle of 'freedom of worship', and thus freedom not to worship, has been firmly established as an inviolable feature of the British democratic way of life for a very long time. It certainly pre-dates the more obvious multicultural and multiracial situations which characterize the life of many major cities in late twentieth-century England. In such a society all religious claims and practices are controversial in nature and, therefore, are freely discussed and debated.

What, then, is the purpose of R.E. in the schools of such a society and what principles are there to guide teachers in their delivery of it in schools?

The following two extracts are from one book on the subject (Read, *et al.*, 1986). They are offered here as stimuli for reflection and discussion.

The Aim and General Principles of Religious Education

The principal aim of Religious Education is to help children mature in relation to their own patterns of belief and behaviour through exploring religious beliefs and practices and related human experiences.

The Seven Principles of R.E.

First Principle:	Children need to develop their own beliefs and values and a consistent pattern of behaviour.
Second Principle:	R.E. has a particularly important contribution to make to the personal and social development of children.
Third Principle:	In R.E. the role of the teacher is that of educator.

Fourth Principle:	As in all other subject areas, the teaching of R.E. must be related to the ages and abilities of the children being taught.
Fifth Principle:	R.E. will help children to explore a range of religious beliefs and practices and related human experiences.
Sixth Principle:	R.E. makes a major contribution to multicultural education.
Seventh Principle:	R.E. does not make assumptions about, or pre-conditions for, the personal commitments of teachers or children.

Presenting Religious Matters
in the Classroom

The concern here is not about the nature and function of so-called 'religious language'. It is to do with ways of talking about and presenting religious matters in an open educational context.

Most experienced teachers are well aware of the need to use words that are meaningful to pupils. For example it is not helpful to use technical religious terms unless their meaning is explained, or to use terms which are beyond the present experience or comprehension level of the pupils. Similarly, difficulties in communication arise when terms which have multiple meanings or have a range of associations are used without detailed explanation. Words like 'meek' and 'father', important within the Christian tradition, may be understood in very different ways depending on their accepted usage among people with whom pupils live and perhaps on the experiences that pupils have had. Terms which produce positive feelings in some people may have negative meanings for others.

However, there are a few other language styles and conventions which are required of teachers when they are presenting religious matters within the context of R.E. A failure to adopt and maintain these conventions often results in both a breakdown in communication and in increasing resentment on the part of many pupils.

While these conventions are essential to the purposes of R.E., they are not unique to it. They are in fact used by most adults when they engage in conversation with others about controversial issues. These are accepted protocols and manners which are used to avoid any appearance of pushing one's own ideas and beliefs 'down someone else's throat'. Adults exercising these protocols endeavour to show respect for each other's views while, at the same time, taking the opportunity to voice, strongly if need be, personally held convictions.

In order to make clear the nature of these conventions and to stress their importance for R.E., we introduce the notion of 'owning and grounding'.

OWNING AND GROUNDING

Central to this need to own or ground belief statements is the distinction between 'fact' and 'belief' types of statement. Among other things, such statements are those about which differences of outlook are found within the community. Particularly in R.E., they include statements about God, claims about religious leaders or interpretations of sacred books. For example, in speaking about Jesus, a distinction may be made between saying that he was crucified at a particular time or place and saying that he was the Christ who died for the sins of the whole world in accordance with God's plan. The first statement could be the factual reporting of any observer and is potentially open to historical research. The latter statement presumes a belief about who Jesus was and thus is of a different kind.

It is possible, indeed it is essential to the purposes of R.E., that both kinds of statements be used in the classroom and that pupils become aware of the distinction between them and skilled in using them appropriately.

Sometimes teachers and pupils may own a particular belief as theirs, by the use of such terms as 'I believe...,' 'It seems to me that...,' 'I feel...,' 'I think...,' or 'In my experience....'

Alternatively they may ground the belief by attaching it to some groups of people who hold it, or to some source from which it comes, for example, 'Muslims believe', or 'It says in the Qur'an', or 'Some/many people do not believe'.

Owning or grounding a belief does not prove or assume that it is true or authoritative for others. However, because it does not presume upon their agreement the pupils are more likely to be able to hear and to discuss what is being presented and may not feel that particular beliefs or values are being forced on them.

When beliefs are owned or grounded they sound less dogmatic, and some may fear they will sound less authoritative. However, when the source of their authority, whether in personal experience or in a tradition, is made clear, this provides important data for those who are being asked to consider where they stand in relation to those beliefs. A quick way to check the authority or source of a belief statement is to ask 'Who says it?' or 'Who believes it?' This assists teachers and/or pupils either to own the statement or to ground it by indicating who believes it to be true.

References

Grimmitt, M. (1978), *What Can I Do In RE?* (Southend-on-Sea: Mc-Crimmon).

Grimmitt, M. (1987), *Religious Education and Human Development* (Southend-on-Sea: McCrimmon).

Holm, J. (1975), *Teaching Religion in School* (London: OUP).

Hull, J. (Ed.) (1982), *New Directions in Religious Education* (Basingstoke: Falmer Press).

Hull, J. (1984), *Studies in Religion and Education* (Basingstoke: Falmer Press).

Read, G. *et al.* (1986), *How Do I Teach RE?* (London: Mary Glasgow Publications).

Watson, B. (1987), *Education and Belief* (Oxford: Basil Blackwell).

Sequel 2   Good Talk

Within the descriptions in this book of each school day, there are many instances in which talk occurs – between teacher and class, teacher and individual or small group, or boys and girls. Talk is the key classroom means by which personal relationships are begun and developed; information is transmitted; investigation is sustained; control is exercised. What, then, is good talk and how may it be identified?

(1)   It is concerned with the ability to communicate well in a variety of situations, formal and informal, personal and public.

(2)   It means being able to express well the thoughts in the mind. This improves with practice and leads to better crystallization of those thoughts and a more secure grasp on ideas. Thus, articulating thoughts helps to preserve them. As the Russian poet Osip Mandelstam says: 'I have forgotten the words I intended to say, and my thoughts, unembodied, return to the realm of shadows.'

(3)   It is functional in expressing emotions, feelings, opinions, ideally, in an honest and unpretentious manner. The language used and the language user are inseparable. Language is, then, not only an indicator of personality; it can also be a medium for therapy.

(4)   It also has the ability to perform other language functions, such as: problem solving; linking cause and effect; substantiating opinions with reasons; observing accurately; predicting consequences; speculating and hypothesizing.

(5)   Good talk is worth listening to. It involves good listening and being aware of the listener's needs. The good speaker empathizes with the listener. For this reason it will involve appropriate switching between registers, dialects – even languages themselves, as well as choice and variation of diction, pace, volume and intonation.

(6)   In addition to such paralinguistic features, good talk will

also involve appropriate physical movements (kinesics) and speaker positions (proxemics).

(7) It involves omission of clichés since these are a substitute for thought. Impoverishment of language correlates with impoverishment of thought. Hence its crucial role in education.

(8) It involves omission of jargon except where such jargon is part of the restricted code of the language community (as here!).

(9) Good talk often necessitates hesitation and use of constructions such as 'er' (and even 'you know', on occasions) in order to allow for verbal planning. It is not the monologue of the museum guide who ploughs on in a vacuum, oblivious to all around.

How do the teachers, whose words are recorded in this book, stand up to such a checklist? How do we ourselves? And if these are to be our aims, how do we develop good talk within our classroom? What kind of structure and atmosphere do we promote which will allow good talk to flourish?

Let's consider the pros and cons of teacher-directed class discussion. Here are some assertions:

Pros	Cons
(a) Encourages a coherent examination of an issue.	(a) Interrogatory style is inimical to real discussion
(b) Allows all to express an opinion or make a contribution.	(b) Little real opportunity for all to participate.
(c) Promotes wide range of expression of different viewpoints.	(c) Little real interplay between children on account of boomerang-style mediation through the teacher.
(d) Common experience develops the sense of class unity and cohesion.	(d) Cohesion is spurious on account of frustration of those unable to contribute adequately.
(e) Teacher in control to protect the weak while restraining the strong.	(e) No leadership initiative and self-reliance permitted to children.
(f) Teacher knows what ground has been covered.	(f) Stress is on product rather than process. There is little opportunity for the language of hypothesis, exploration, speculation.

What, then, of the prospective value of paired or small group discussion? Here are some more assertions:

Pros	Cons
(a) More children speak.	(a) Noise level is high.
(b) More opportunity for leadership of a transferable kind, with shifting exercise of a variety of roles.	(b) Weak children suffer.
(c) Intimate context more appropriate for expressive language in which to describe feelings, opinions, beliefs, attitudes.	(c) Any insights gained are not relayed to larger class.
(d) Children get to know each other well.	(d) The contact is merely social and could equally take place in the playground.
(e) Children determine their own agenda, within the constraints imposed by the task or situation.	(e) Discussion is low level.
(f) Children are free to use appropriate register, accent, dialect, mother tongue.	(f) Language used is not understood by wider community,

Perhaps such a dichotomy is false, because real classroom life, as opposed to theoretical constructs, will involve a mixing of modes, and many instances of public and private utterance. Certainly, children need much experience of both and it may be worth examining the days described in the book from the perspective of the language experience which is being mediated.

Finally, as part of the process of 'learning to listen to language', here are some comments made by students in training, after they had scrutinized a transcript of one of their lessons. See if you can place them under one (or more) of these five headings, as an indication of the area in which the student's awareness increased:

(1) Proportions of talk.
(2) Own teaching style.
(3) Questioning technique.
(4) Knowledge of individuals.
(5) Language process.

(a)   'In seven minutes, eighteen children were asked or offered answers to questions and seventeen gave answers. This is approximately two-thirds of the class present on that day' (Joy, with 9-year-olds).

(b)   'My question, "Can anyone suggest how we might go about it?" is an open question to get them to include their own original ideas' (Elizabeth, with 8-year-olds).

(c)   Said of one boys' contribution: 'He is thinking as he is talking, and forming his conversation around disjointed thoughts' (Rod, with 9-year-olds).

(d)   'The transcript highlights the fact that the discussion is completely directed from the teacher. There is little pupil initiation or pupil to pupil interaction, (Amy, with forty 7-year-olds).

(e)   'The way in which the lesson was set up and carried out conveys the basic assumption that I am the fountain of all knowledge and that they must accept the factual information passively. This, I admit, is disturbing' (James, with 9-year-olds).

(f)   'The transcript shows I allowed Ian to have attention when he constantly demanded it. This was because he is brain-damaged and does not always readily enter into discussions, as he usually finds the level of conversation too high for him' (Juliana, with 8-year-olds).

(g)   'She is using her own language and not bothering to adapt it for the teacher' (says Steve, of 8-year-old Jane's description of 'horrible, sweaty, smelly pigs and stinking hens').

(h)   'This pupil (nicknamed by the other children "Rent-a-mouth") was just being silly here. I don't think he can help talking a lot; he just blurts it out and then apologizes' (Bruce, with 10-year-olds).

(i)   'My instructions are very unclear when I think about them afterwards...I find I'm always asking them if they understand. This is probably distracting for them' (Monika, with 10-year-olds).

(j)   'There were thirty children present and only seven were involved in the discussion. I should have brought more in' (Alan, with 9-year-olds).

(k)   'Reading through the transcript I notice that I have not really acknowledged the answers I was given, apart from repeating them so all children can hear. At times I could have extended the children's answers' (John, with 9 to 11-year-olds).

(l) 'The questions are mostly closed, and serve the purpose of recalling information but do not in themselves allow for an expansion of the facts or for exploratory communication' (Anne, with forty 7-year-olds).

(m) 'I did not realize until I taped this, that all the questions came from me and not from the children' (Hugh, with 9-year-olds).

(n) 'Teacher reinforces answer with "Yes", then twists it into what she really wanted the children to say' (Marion, with 7-year-olds).

(o) 'Very perceptive child who doesn't take one of the leading roles in the group. She relates back to me a lot instead of to the rest of the group' (Alison, referring to 10-year-old Amanda).

Finally, a brief exchange which defies categorization.

Picture the scene: student teacher Helen, talking with a class of 7-year-olds about silk worms.

Lee: Jesus tries to make cruel people kind people, doesn't he?
Helen: Yes.
Lee: It just won't work with Dracula.

Sequel 3   Teacher Training Tasks

Chapter 1. Mike

(1) As a lively and interesting extrovert, Mike is potentially disruptive. How does Mrs Hilton contain and harness his energies? Are her methods your methods?

(2) At one point in the morning, the children in Mike's group who have plastic objects for maths work use them in a game of Cowboys and Indians. Would you allow this in your class? Why or why not?

(3) What opportunities do the children in the class have to talk about their own experience? How can such opportunities be valuable to them?

(4) How much religious influence does there appear to be during Mike's day and how is this illuminated by Sequel 1?

(5) How much social class influence is there and of what kind is it?

(6) How much moral influence is there and of what kind is it? It may be helpful, in this regard, to refer to six moral education categories, that is, the ability to:

(a) treat others with consideration;
(b) understand and identify with the feelings of others;
(c) master the facts relevant to the making of moral decisions;
(d) formulate social rules in relation to society;
(e) make rules for one's personal conduct;
(f) put these into practice.

(See J. Wilson (1967), *Introduction to Moral Education*, Penguin).

Clearly, these education categories will be achieved, if at all, at different stages and ages. In what practical ways could each of them be appreciated by infants and by juniors?

How may the infant, and junior, school, by organization and network of relationships, contribute to this moral development of the individual?

(7)   The children in Mike's class hear, or sing, a number of rhymes and songs throughout the day. What is the value of this? Which rhymes and songs are popular with children you know? Why do you think these are particularly popular?

(8)   The transcribed exchanges between Mrs Hilton and her class could be subjected to all kinds of analysis. You might look particularly at:
   (a) the approximate proportions of teacher/pupil talk;
   (b) the specific language style (that is, idiolect) of Mrs Hilton, in so far as this can be determined from a transcript;
   (c) the kinds of questions asked and the ways in which they are asked;
   (d) the variety of purposes for which language is used;
   (e) the roles of teacher and pupils involved.

(9)   In writing of the cultural ingredients in the educational process, Basil Bernstein draws a distinction between the 'instrumental' and the 'expressive'. Instrumental refers to the acquisition of specific skills, and expressive relates to the transmission of models of 'conduct, character and manner'.
   Try to distinguish between these two elements of cultural transmission in the description of Mike's day (or of any other day in the book). At what points, if any, do they appear to overlap?

(10) Look again at the seven principles of R.E. in Sequel 1. Which of these principles would also be appropriate for which other curriculum areas?

(11) According to King (1978), 'It is possible to distinguish a number of important elements that comprise the infant teacher's child-centred ideology. These are: developmentalism, individualism, play as learning, and childhood innocence.'
   What evidence for the existence of these four elements do you find in Chapter 1?

Chapter Two

Rashda, Aged 6

I saw the Indian no [sic] television

The School

Rashda attends a large infants school of 350 children in a now decaying, residential suburb of an industrial city. Gradually, the poorer Edwardian houses are being demolished and replaced by smart council houses and flats. In this area the school is a focus for stability, although the demolition and rebuilding, with concomitant change and mobility, produces constant alterations on the school roll. Not merely in the names of the children attending, but in their ethnic origins and social backgrounds. It is not unknown for stray dogs to roam the streets and rubbish dumps, but the school itself forms something of an oasis, with its neatly laid out gardens and buildings contrasting markedly with the nearby untidy railway yard, where lorries off-load scrap. Not far away can be seen small factories and metal-smelting works.

The main school building is twenty-five years old, and a number of mobile classrooms and a nursery unit of fifty places have been added more recently. Eleven infants staff are complemented by three and a half extra teachers who cope with special remedial reading classes and English as a Second Language, the only occasions when children are grouped according to their ability.

The school intake is composed of 20 per cent white children, a slightly smaller proportion of children with West Indian origins, and a majority of children whose origins are Asian. In the main, these are of Sikh background, but there are also some Gujeratis, some Pakistanis, and some Indian Christians.

The Day

It is 9.00a.m. on a fine, cold autumn day and the children whose turn it is (that is, about half of all those in the school) have come straight into assembly, by-passing their classrooms, many fully dressed in coats and anoraks. This is one way of saving useful time in the school day. The hall seems large because the children are so small, sitting cross-legged in rows, with the choir on a dais, facing inwards towards the teacher in the middle, who is to conduct the assembly.

Rashda is pointed out to me, sitting with a smile, gripping one of the legs of the chair which the teacher of English as a Second Language is sitting on. Her name indicates Muslim culture. The family originated in the sub-continent, but Rashda herself was born in England. She is rather chubby, with dark eyes and black hair, done in two plaits, tied with orange ribbons. A fringe on her forehead sticks up as though it has just been washed. She is well dressed in a dark purple trouser suit, partially covered by a green cardigan. Her shoes are black, yellow and green. I am told that she had been ill the day before with earache.

The assembly teacher now asks, in a very quiet voice, to see everyone's hands. Silence descends immediately. It is a simple but highly effective ploy, and some such method is needed by all teachers, particularly when handling large numbers of children. She now asks to see everyone's face.

Teacher: Put down everything in your hands. (*They do so*.) Good morning, children.
Children: Good morning, Miss Francis.
Teacher: Good morning, everyone.
Children: Good morning, everyone.

After this formal and courteous beginning, we sing a hymn which, from one point of view if not another, might be thought appropriate for a multi-ethnic school. The children are accompanied by a member of staff on the piano.

> Jesus loves the little children,
> All the children of the world;
> Red and yellow, black and white,

All are precious in his sight,
Jesus loves the little children of the world.

Teacher: Hands together. Eyes closed. (*They do so.*)
            Let us pray together and work together to make our
            school and the world a happy, lovely place.
            Think of the children in your class and the teachers
            and the ladies about the school. Mr Morgan. The lol-
            lipop lady. Your mummies and daddies and nannies.[1]
            (*A coin drops.*) Amen.
Children: Amen.
Teacher: Do you all think of ways you can help people? Yes?
Children: Yes.
Teacher: Well, I shall be round the school all day, seeing if
            you are helping people. And, Class 10, *All day!*

This injunction to good behaviour is reinforced by the next
hymn, with the children performing appropriate hand movements.

The wise man built his house upon the rock   *(Children place
The wise man built his house upon the rock   fist on fist)*
The wise man built his house upon the rock
And the rain came tumbling down.   *(Hand-waving motion)*

The rain came down and the floods came up   *(Outstretched
The rain came down and the floods came up   fingers moved
The rain came down and the floods came up   up in stages)*
And the house on the rock stood firm.   *(Fist on fist)*

---

1   One could legitimately expect the children to understand this prayer, since its
concerns are close to their experience and they know the people being referred
to. One might even speculate on whether the reference to 'nannies' is intended
to reflect the extended family influences which many of the children here will
be familiar with. Often the language of prayers in school may represent sheer
confusion to many young children. Witness the 6-year-old who prayed:

> Thy deliberately faith I full,
> Faith against almight worship God,
> And faith all unto you,
> Faith against they holy prayer.
> (Goldman, R. J., 1964, *Religious Thinking from
> Childhood to Adolescence*, Routledge & Kegan Paul.)

It is a kind of computer's prayer, gone wrong.

The foolish man built his house upon the sand *(Waving hands)*
The foolish man built his house upon the sand
The foolish man built his house upon the sand
And the rain came tumbling down.   *(Hand-waving motion)*

The rain came down and the floods came up   *(Outstretched*
The rain came down and the floods came up   *fingers again)*
The rain came down and the floods came up
And the house on the sand fell FLAT!   *(Loud clap)*

The loud clap, made by everyone with great enthusiasm, marks the end of the assembly.

Teacher: You're going to have to watch me very carefully to see if your class should go out. (*She signals to one boy who stands up.*) If you're in the same class as this boy, stand up. (*No one moves.*) What class are you in?
Boy: Class 7.
Teacher: Oh! You shouldn't be here anyway. Off you go.

The routine is repeated, with rather more success, and one class goes out to the words and music of 'Baa Baa Black Sheep'; another to a verse from 'Humpty Dumpty', and so on.

Apart from the establishment of a respectful atmosphere, the sense of corporate identity and individual concern, and the calming influence at the beginning of the day, the assembly may well have achieved other aims too. Notice the valuable language activities which have occurred – the co-ordination of hand movements with appropriate words; the enjoyment of rhythm and repetition; the simple narrative with a clear sequence and ending; the reinforcement of verbs in the past tense; the reminder of well-loved rhymes, which are a part of the English cultural heritage.

There is time to ponder on this a little now in the classroom as the children queue outside. The room is quite large, with windows on two sides, one side frosted and the other looking out on to the playground. There is a play house in one corner and reading materials, including a lockable cupboard full of books, in another. A nature table contains a picture book about THE BULB, and labels such as BLACKBIRD'S NEST; ROSEHIPS; LAUREL; TANGY; GRANDFATHER; BLACKBERRIES.

Around the walls are various pieces of equipment and school work, including self-portraits with the children's names, to make identification possible; butterfly cut-outs, made and coloured by the children; a teacher-made colour chart with lists of months of the year, days of the week, and words for a story (such as: *girl, boy, witch, wizard, giant, castle, king, queen, prince, princess*). There is also a list of words with significant parts highlighted. For example:

hot   not
got   dog

In each case, the short *o* is printed in a different colour from that of the other letters. Its pronounciation is exactly the same in the four words listed which suggests a stress on phonics in the teaching of reading in the school. As further support for this material, there is a professionally produced alphabet chart, with letter, plus word, plus drawing.

There is a table of maths materials, including boxes of work cards, counting equipment, magnets, model clocks, toys such as 'Lego', and a cupboard of children's boxes, each neatly labelled with their names, and containing their own work. Also a cupboard of open shelves, with scissors, paper handkerchiefs, chalk, rulers, etc. Such equipment can serve as the springboard for a child's interest, or the facilitator of a task in progress. A stimulus balance is necessary.

The teacher's desk is at the front of the room, to the side of the blackboard, and the tables are arranged in six groups each with six chairs and one line of pencils.

A boy comes into the room and looks at my notebook. 'All the boys and girls', he says, even though that is not what I have written. Strangely enough, he said exactly the same thing a week earlier, when I came on a preliminary visit. Doubtless, it is his way of drawing attention to himself and establishing some kind of contact.

The rest of the children now enter, leaving their coats on a rack outside the classroom door. They sit on a mat in front of Mrs Parsons, a slim, quietly spoken teacher in her mid-20s, who now calls the attendance register, boys first, followed by the girls.

Mrs P.: Joseph ... Stephen ... Sukhjinder ... Raj ... Peter ...
        Amarjit ... (*and so on*).
        Inderjit ... Dawn ... Kuldip ... Jenny ... (*and so on*).[1]

---

1 *A Guide to Asian Names* is available free on request from the Commission for Racial Equality, Elliott House, 10/12 Allington Street, London SW1E 5EH. Tel. 01 828 7022. CRE also publishes a monthly broadsheet.

Thirty in all, and in each case the child answers, 'Yes, Miss Parsons', not considered inappropriate for a married lady.

The practical purpose of calling the register is to identify absentees. Part of the hidden curriculum of such a ritual may well be to heighten the significance of the occasion, and to help develop a corporate identity, by making pupils more aware, if only slightly, of their classmates and, maybe, of gender differences, too.

During the marking of the dinner register there is a knock at the door and Tina enters, carrying a small brown bag which had been left in the hall by one of the boys. Some schools seem to have a constant traffic in such messengers, for a variety of purposes. Perhaps to find lost owners, or lost articles; to bring items of news; trace a boy or a girl; check dinner numbers; advertise school events. The interruptions may be annoying for some teachers, and time-wasting for some pupils, selected because they are nuisances. On the credit side, are the potentially beneficial effects on the messengers trusted with the task. In any event, the transactions of any institution must go forward and, short of installing a classroom intercom system (such as is done in the occasional large secondary school), there seem few practical alternatives to human message-carriers.

Soon registers give way to more exciting possibilities, as the teacher says: 'Have any of you got raffle ticket money before you go?' One child has, and he pays up. Then Rashda and five others are off to a small annexe for thirty minutes of English as a Second Language, i.e. special daily language work for those children whose grip on English is tenuous or non-existent. Many live in at least two language worlds and switch from one language to another, when met at the school gates each day, perhaps twice a day, by parents or relatives. However adaptable and resilient, as children are traditionally supposed to be, one wonders at the effect on them of such abrupt transitions. What , too, of the effects on their parents?

The annexe is a cramped and cold space, partitioned off outside a classroom, but made to look attractive with plenty of pictures on the walls, cut-out figures, books, objects, a clock, and a weather chart. The language teacher, Mrs Matthews, a member of the city's peripatetic team, but based at this school all the week, is a slim, medium-sized, dark-haired person in her late 20s, with a quiet and efficient style.

First, there is a brief preliminary chat about the days of the week and the weather that day. Such talk of the weather may help to develop language and powers of observation by sensitizing children to their environment. At this stage the language is simple and the judgement global, for example: 'It is raining'; 'It is sunny'.

After this initial acclimatization for the children, the main part of the session begins. It is a revision lesson to reinforce language structures involving the words *on*, *in*, and *under*. Each time a phrase is used it is highlighted by an action with an object, and the six children sitting round the table are consistently involved; the girls – Rashda, Inderjit and Kuldip and the boys – Alwis, Sukhjinder and Balvant.

The children obviously enjoy the session and are highly motivated, participating constantly. One can almost chart Rashda's progress, from uncertainty and diffidence, to a rather more secure understanding of the structures being revised, even though they are not yet entirely grasped. The teacher energetically moves about, relating language structure to meaningful action. She adopts the systematic structural/situational approach to second language learning which would be endorsed by many experienced in this field. If the structures are clearly established, so the argument runs, then varying items of vocabulary may be slotted in as required.

There is regular reward ('right', 'good', 'yes') and repetition of the structure to be taught, where the teacher's own language must necessarily be very precise and uniform. It would be matey but confusing to say to a child: 'Now, I don't suppose you can tell me what this is, can you, me old friend?' Imagine yourself as a second language learner, trying to cope with that in, say, Russian, or Serbo-Croat.

After revision of *in* and *on*, Mrs Matthews moves on to the word *under* and now asks each child: 'Where are your hands?'; Where are your legs?' Alwis makes an interesting and acute observation. 'Like cutting', he says, 'like cut hands', indicating that his own hands have been 'cut off' under the table. It is what might be termed 'creative talk', based on real perception.

Then, the same procedure as earlier follows, with objects (for example, a bin) and picture cards. This time, by using the present continuous tense, a greater narrative element can be introduced.

This leads naturally to a more extended narrative and the popular story, in the illustrated 'Ladybird' version, of the three goats in which, you will recall, the troll lived under the bridge ... under the bridge ... under the bridge. Balwant, perhaps rather afraid of the picture of the ugly troll, says, 'He could that one could bash him up in the water'. It is one of several indications in this lesson of how non-English speakers call upon other sources for the language they use. Perhaps the comment reflects playground talk.

After more repetition of *under*, in various contexts, Mrs Matthews moves to the next phase of the lesson, again intended as reinforcement. The children are now required to complete drawings on cyclostyled sheets, putting a brown dog *under* the table ... a blue book *under* the chair ... a black cat *under* the television. As they complete the sheet, working quite co-operatively in exchanging coloured crayons, they have an opportunity to practise rather different kinds of language, that is, instrumental for getting jobs done, and interactional, in the social context.

All through the lesson Rashda has been concentrating and involved, enjoying each different activity, and making oral contributions on no less than forty-one separate occasions. So many more comments than would have been possible in a full class, and highlighting one of the advantages of such small group language work.

Their daily half-hour lesson is over, and they return to their classroom as Mrs Matthews prepares for the next six.

Rashda is now (that is, at 9.55 a.m.) back with her original class, this time sitting in a group around three double desks with Jindo, Balwant, Dawn, Narrinder and Darryl. Virtually all the children in the class are quite well dressed and appear to be well cared for. There are two girl twins of West Indian origin, identically clothed in yellow dresses, grey cardigans, black shoes, blue socks, white ribbons in their hair. There are two West Indian boys; six English girls; one English boy; and the remainder of the children are of Indian and Pakistani origin. The atmosphere in the classroom is of purposeful activity as the children copy from the blackboard sentences intended to reinforce work they had done with Mrs Parsons on the *i* sound, and the distinction between *i* and *j*. Some children are sitting working; others half standing; others kneeling; others waiting around the teacher's desk to have their work checked.

Rashda, with one shoe on and one off, struggles with flagging concentration. She has copied the teacher's sentences, but has not invented any of her own, which was part of the exercise. As an aid to invention and retention, each of the children has a small, alphabetically arranged, word book in which to put words they encounter, with each letter having a separate page.

Rashda looks at her word book and asks others in her group to read words to her, which they do. Such co-operation is a common feature of the class, as is unsolicited entertainment. 'Look!' exclaims Darryl, 'I've got a loose tooth', and, with a tentative stabbing movement, proves his words to the admiration of two onlookers. Sometimes the bustle and activity exceed educational limits. 'Er, Joseph, if I have to speak to you once more ... ', says Mrs Parsons. The incomplete, unspecified threat is effective, and silence descends for a while.

It is 10.17a.m. and Rashda goes off to stand in the queue for teacher's desk. There are eight children in front of her. Her work is shortly checked and Mrs Parsons stands with her hands up, palms outwards, and says, 'Children!' The children copy her actions and silence reigns in a second, as though vocal and physical systems are linked. The same superbly effective method, you will recall, occurred in assembly and it is interesting to find evidence of a common approach throughout the school. While every teacher will have her own range of such invaluable devices for calling her group to attention without undue fuss and noise, if colleagues share the same methods they are likely to be more powerful.

There is generally a clear relationship between teacher's noise level and class's noise level. One provokes the other in an ever-increasing spiral of decibels. Quiet teachers often make for quiet classes. Mrs Parsons explains quietly that the children are to put their books in their tables and prepare for their drinks, which they do.

Rashda now sits with arms folded, straining backward, with the index finger of her left hand on her lips, presumably exhorting everyone else to silence. No other child adopts this position.

Now there is industry of a different kind as the children sit sucking their drinks and eating biscuits and sweets. Concentration never wavers until all is gone. Such rituals are the medium by which social learning occurs. As R. S. Peters comments

(1966): 'Rituals as well as the use of authority are a method by means of which the importance of a practice can be marked out and children made to feel that it is something in which they should participate.'

What characterizes a ritual seems to be consistency of detail, repetition of operation, with the understanding on the part of all participants (or, perhaps, on occasions, the teacher only) that its enactment has some other kind of outcome. There is, in other words, a prospective power behind the present action. 'Children have to be initiated into forms of thought and behaviour, the rationale of which they cannot at first properly understand' (Peters, 1966). Hence the devices described throughout this book for gaining attention, exerting authority, organising children, enlisting participation and involvement, locating the individual within the community. A perfect example of this last device will be found in the next chapter.

The children on Rashda's table now show each other how to sit with arms folded, and again she adopts her individual Buddha-like stance before skipping to sit on the mat in the same manner. Mrs Parsons hands her a work book; she reads the name on it and takes it to its owner. It is a subtle way for reading practice to have an immediate practical outcome.

More children now have finished their lunch and are occupying the mat in front of the teacher, who sits in her chair holding the hand of a boy at her side. Some children mill around the classroom coat rack, collecting anoraks before joining the others on the mat. To see them squashed together, but uncomplaining, on this small piece of territory reminds one momentarily of ominous visual representations, seen from time to time on television, warning of overpopulation.

That thought flits by as one of the boys spontaneously begins to sing 'One two three four five, Once I caught a fish alive', and the song is taken up by several others. When it is over, there are a few moments of silence as we wait for the bell. It sounds and, one by one, the children are given permission to go to the playground. On her way, one of the girls says to me, 'My big sister ... after Father Christmas ... we got toy roof ... ' but we shall never really know what information she intended to convey. Another girl endows me with all her worldly goods, 3p, saying that unless I guard it 'someone will pinch it'. She will retrieve it after the danger of breaktime is past.

Mrs Parsons is on playground duty and has arranged for another member of staff to provide coffee. Mrs Heal duly arrives with the coffee and tells me of the interest aroused among the children by the tall sunflower which one of the teachers has been growing just outside in the garden. Apparently some of the children who have seen it talk of Jack and the Beanstalk, and I heard later that this innocent gardening idea had blossomed into a means of raising money for the school fund. Each child who participated in the scheme backed a sunflower seed for 2p. Named pegs in the ground linked seeds with their promoters and, at the end of a prescribed period of time, the backer of the tallest sunflower won the prize of a packet of felt-tipped pens and a colouring book. Not only did the scheme raise attractive sunflowers, useful money and considerable interest in growing things, it also gave the children opportunities for estimation and measurement in a matter close to their hearts.

The classroom is now empty of children, enclosed in a kind of echoing silence, heightened by the morning's bustle. The sounds of the playground – distant screams and muted shouts – can be heard over against the noises of metal being dumped and lorries unloaded. Schools and classrooms are dead places without their occupants.

At 10.55 a.m. the children are back in class and the special needs teacher has arrived to collect a group of six, of whom Rashda is one, for a short period of concentrated attention on reading. Mrs Renshaw is a teacher in her late 20s, of medium height and with auburn hair and freckles. She has a quiet voice and a warm manner. Off we go to another mobile classroom and, before the lesson proper begins, the children slide their ink-well tops backwards and forwards, chanting 'close ... open ... close ... open'.

Mrs Renshaw begins some letter recognition work. She holds up a card and the children call out the sound of the letter displayed: *a ... buh ... kuh ... duh ... e*. Next she uses a collection of neat, home-produced, pink cards, each with a drawing and a label: *dog, axe, egg, ambulance, boy, doll, elephant, baby, car, boats, arrow, bee, duck*. As each card is displayed and named, so the children cover up the corresponding picture on their larger master card which has eight sections. It is a form of word bingo, as the children soon indicate.

At first Rashda does not see what is required of her but watches the others and soon grasps the idea. She does not shout

out 'I've got ... ', as others do, but quietly consults her card and looks at the cards of those near her. After one or two rounds the children take over from the teacher as callers and Rashda has her turn. '*kuh* for cat', she says, '*a* for apple' (and is corrected when the word is seen to be *ambulance*); '*duh* for dog; *kuh* for clock; *buh* for baby' (the picture is, in fact, of a boy).

She is guessing the formula without reading the words and needs help at breaking down a word into its constituent parts, something in which there will be practice later in the day back in normal classwork. In any event, it needs to be done carefully, so as to avoid the pitfall of separately pronouncing distinct elements which then do not add up to a proper word. *Duh ... o ... guh* does not add up to the word *dog*. If the method is to be used at all – and it may well assist good spelling and interest in words – it should be employed at the appropriate time, and not forced on children before they can cope with such phoneme separation. Bullock (1975) is wary and believes that we should go back to using traditional rhymes and jingles (such as were seen in abundance in Chapter 1). The Report's words, in para. 6.17, are worth quoting:

> What the variations within each phoneme have in common is some kind of preparatory position in the speaker's vocal apparatus, but this configuration changes as the sound is produced, depending on which sound is to follow. If, then, we teach a child how to pronounce a series of sounds and ask him to run them together to form a word he will indeed learn the trick of saying those separate sounds and of then saying the related word. But he has certainly not built up the word from the sounds he has pronounced first ... The process is not yet fully understood by which children learn to imitate the sounds of speech and discriminate between them. To break up a word into what are thought to be its constituent elements does not, however, seem to us the best means of developing this process. We believe a better way is for teachers to rely upon methods that have a long history in the infant school but which have unaccountably fallen out of favour; namely, the use of rhymes, jingles and alliteration. These focus attention on the contrastive elements in words while avoiding the inevitable distortions of the more analytic approach.

Meanwhile, Rashda continues to make every effort. She is quietly confident and assured, and smiles each time she reads a word. There is no fuss when she makes an error. The children, as a group, are very keen and enthusiastic, often guessing words (e.g. *egg* for *elephant*). They are sharply competitive, each being concerned to win, and this is where the emphasis of the session falls, rather than on the actual reading. So much so, that occasionally feeling runs high, as in this seemingly Old Testament confrontation:

Joshua: You was teasing me.
Joseph: I weren't teasing you, you liar.
Joshua: You was.
Joseph: I weren't teasing you, you liar.
Joshua: You shut up.
Joseph: I don't have to.
Joshua: You shut up.

Having reached this impasse, the rest was, fortunately, inaudible on the tape.

At 11.10 a.m. the last round of the word bingo finished, with three simultaneous winners, and it is time to move on: 'Put your chairs [*sic*] and don't forget your watch, Surinder. Off you go.'

The children move to rejoin the rest of the class, who are now sitting on steps in the school foyer, watching the end of a television programme for schools, about a carpenter who is making a zither. The children participate by singing the words of the chorus, performing appropriate actions, such as sawing and hammering, and clapping in time to the music at the end of the programme.

The last verse is rendered inaudible by the movement of other children, but it includes notes from the new zither.

Announcer: Do you know what the carpenter was making? It's a zither (*she plucks the strings*). You have to be a very good carpenter to make a zither.
Singer: But you could try making a splinter. (*He demonstrates the sound of this simple instrument.*)
Announcer: Or a pair of claves. (*Again a demonstration.*)
Singer: And you could make a Jingling Johnny too. (*Another demonstration.*)
Announcer: And then you could use them all to accompany the carpenter's song.

	Goodbye.
Singer:	Goodbye.
Children:	Goodbye. (*Music plays out the programme.*)

Television can be such a gripping medium that children are often completely captivated by a programme, good or mediocre. Precisely what value a programme has is difficult to determine. Often they seem to be interludes within the school day, unrelated to anything else, but they can be used as a springboard for a variety of creative activities, or as a booster to work in progress.

Rashda and her peers seem to enjoy the singing in the zither programme but one doubts its further language and cultural value, although the repetition of *say, hammer, bore, turn,* may help the non-English-speaking children. Clearly, no child here will be in a position to make the rather exotic musical instruments mentioned at the end, although older children might.

It is now 11.18 a.m. The boys and girls line up separately and walk back to the classroom, where they continue with the sentences which they were previously working on, rather than use the opportunity to follow up parts of the television programme. Perhaps they will do so on another occasion, although infant memory spans are short.

Rashda is having her work checked at the teacher's desk. She is actually with Mrs Parsons for forty-five seconds and returns with two ticks against the sentences she has copied, but still without having written any of her own. A word from me to her:

R. M.:	Where's your Daddy?
	(*No reply.*)
	Is he at the factory?
	(*She nods her head.*)
	Where's your Mummy?
Rashda:	At home.

She now writes: 'I saw Indian' in her book and returns to stand in the queue near the teacher's desk. I look at her number book while she is away and another girl, ever vigilant, asks me: 'Have you copied them?

After three minutes in the queue Rashda returns to her desk merely to write her name on her word book before rejoining the teacher queue.

54

Shortly afterwards she returns with the word *television* in her alphabet book and this enables her to complete the sentence, 'I saw the Indian no [*sic*] television', in a few seconds before returning to the teacher's desk yet again, this time with ten children to be seen before her.

I later queried this procedure with another teacher on the staff, who operated in a similar manner herself, although she had never done so in her previous school. She maintained that if she moved around the class from table to table, then it had a Pied Piper effect and children wandered about after her. At least if she was at her desk, she felt, they all knew where to find her. So, despite the apparent time-wasting involved, the staff clearly felt such a procedure was right for that school.

One boy in the queue says, 'Thomas, Thomas', and, having caught that boy's attention, dramatically stabs himself with a pencil and, in best Old Vic tradition, 'dies' on the carpet. No one is unduly disturbed by his demise; some children are mildly amused and merely smile. Perhaps he expires in this way quite often.

Some children are now doing addition sums from arithmetic work cards prepared by the teacher; others are still engaged on their sentences. Individuals make a point of checking on my movements. A girl approaches, looks at my notepad, satisfies herself there is no danger, and goes away again. A boy keeps wandering near chanting, 'I'm going by again'. One girl confides, 'Sometimes I get my sums wrong because I've got the wrong number'. A boy counters, 'Today I got them all right'. In the role of teacher, a girl asks, 'Are you doing your homework?' The situation is not unlike that of the anthropologist, who descends with camera and notebook on unknown peoples, to be treated with friendliness and mild amusement.

After three minutes Rashda has had her work marked. The *no* has been changed to *on* and a tick given. One is reminded of the 'pattern practice' for the prepositions *in* and *on* earlier in this chapter during the ESL lesson, and of the three mistakes which Rashda made when using these words. Clearly, the differentiation between the prepositions *in* and *on*, and between the letter sequences *on* and *no* has not yet been established beyond all doubt.

She spends a moment at her own desk and then returns, for reason unknown, to the teacher. Perhaps she needs constant reassurance and contact; perhaps her concentration is waning;

perhaps she has become inextricably involved in an unthinking process.

This time five others are in front of her, and the teacher is working steadily, thoroughly and unhurriedly. The children in the queue are generally well behaved, only one or two occasionally pushing or remonstrating. Others crowd around Mrs Parsons, leaning on her desk as she helps an individual. Two boys in another part of the room are sword-fighting with pencils. Without pausing in her work, and apparently viewing them with eyes in the top of her head, Mrs Parsons says gently, 'Joseph, what have you got there? Come and give me that book', and the combat is over.

Rashda returns after four minutes this time, with a sentence to copy: *I saw an insect crawling on a leaf.* Seconds later it has been done and back she goes, nine children in front of her. Quite clearly, she enjoys the queue.

At this point Mrs Parsons says, 'Children!' She holds up her hands. The children follow suit and again this piece of magic has brought instant quiet. The sixteen dinner children come out to sit on the mat for a minute, before going off to school dinner, while the others are allowed a little more time to finish their work. The mat has been established by custom in this classroom with distinct territorial status. However crowded this magic carpet becomes when the whole class is grouped on it together, no children will tolerate being so cut off that they have no physical contact with even a small part of it. There is power in the connection and the child who was adrift would feel an outsider, cut off from the life-raft. That seems to be one of its functions. To define, and thereby strengthen, a sense of corporateness. At other times it is a kind of staging post or launching pad, from which the children move to other activities. They appear to benefit from the security of a clearly understood logistic routine, and there is orderliness in this classroom without excessive, or even overt, inhibition. As adults, of course, we like our own territory to be clearly defined. Hence our habit of often occupying the same seat in a lecture room or church. The place seems to confirm our identity or, at the least, give us a familiar bearing on our surroundings.

It is now very quiet. Four or five children are working at their desks; six are queuing for the teacher; two or three are around me. One of these reads his own name on his book, three times: 'Jaswan Singh ... Jaswan Singh ... Jaswan Singh.' He is actually called

Peter! When asked what he is to have for dinner, he replies, 'Pachati [presumably, chapati] and curry and tomatoes'.

Rashda is now with Mrs Parsons who elicits from her, with help, the sentence: *I put the milk into the jug.* Each word is said out loud as it is written in her book. Again the same sequence: return to desk; few seconds of copying; back to queue; now three children ahead of her.

This kind of activity and attainment clearly places Rashda in the fifth stage of what Gloyn and Frobisher (1975) identify as a progression of five stages of writing for children in a reception or vertically grouped class. Their description of this copy-writing stage indicates, however, Rashda's tenuous grip, as yet, on the activities normally associated with this stage

> where children draw and colour interesting pictures, have a lot to say about their pictures and can copy reasonably accurately. The 'news' or 'free expression' book is supplemented by copy-writing in maths and as part of the reading programme. There are also many opportunities for children to communicate through writing when pictures and models are displayed.

The Schools Council 'Breakthrough to Literacy' material offers ideal opportunities for such an experience-based approach to reading and writing.

I ask Rashda what she is to have at home for dinner and, after some hesitation, she quietly offers: 'Meat ... carrots ... drink water.'

R. M.:   Are you going to have potatoes?
Rashda: Potato in the carrots.

She says 'Bye bye', and is off home.

It would be easy to calculate the number of minutes Rashda spent merely waiting for Mrs Parsons to check her work, and to assume that all such time had been wasted. It may have been. However, perhaps one could also argue that Rashda's concentration was, in any event, flagging as the morning wore on; that she would not have been able to sustain any more solitary effort; and that queueing up with other children has socializing benefits.

Dinner of sausage, chips, beans, bakewell tart and custard. I sit on a table of five reception-class children who regard me with awe. Ultimately, their fondness for beans overcomes their wonder but, even while eating, they continue to stare with silent inscrutability and my attempts at conversation fail.

1.30p.m. The door of the classroom bursts open and, in a second, the children spill inside, full of life and vigour and, presumably, dinner. They put their coats on hooks and sit on the mat, preparing to answer their names. One or two children arrive late, looking rather pleased. The girls' names follow the boys' and, when this ritual is over, all on the mat turn to face the blackboard on which are written two letters together – *sm* – as a starter for some phonic work.

Mrs Parsons asks for words beginning with *sm* and the first three suggested are: *mouse, Samuel, mud*. Then a child offers the word *smile* and this is written on the board. Next comes *smoke* and then Rashda suggests *something*.

Mrs P.:	'Something?' No, the letters aren't next to each other. Sukhjinder?
Sukhjinder:	Smith.
Mrs P.:	Yes, that's somebody's name, isn't it?
Child:	Smudge, because my Auntie Ellen at the shop has a cat called Smudge.
Mrs P.:	Oh! and that's the cat's name. Yes. Good.
Joseph:	Snow.
Mrs P.:	'Snow?' What letter is that?
Joseph:	suh.
Mrs P.:	suh and a nuh, isn't it?
Child:	Smell.
Child:	Dr Smith.
Child:	Small.
Mrs P.:	'Small'. Good girl.
Child:	Smack.
Peter:	Smack on your botties. (*Several children chuckle.*) Dr Smith.
Mrs P.:	We've had that three times now, you're not listening. Thomas?
Thomas:	Sums.
Mrs P.:	No. You're not thinking now.

At the end of the activity, which lasts about three minutes, the children repeat with Mrs Parsons all the words on the blackboard, going down the list and emphasising the *sm* sound: *SMile* ... *SMoke* ... *SMudge* ... *SMack* ... *SMell* ... *SMall*. It is work to which they will evidently return, time and time again, since the sound is by no means clearly identified by the children.

Next, the teacher holds up a pencilled drawing on cardboard of a prospective puppet of various geometrical shapes, and questions are asked for three or four minutes about these shapes.

Mrs P.:   What shape is his face, Sukhjinder? What shape is his face?
Sukhjinder: Round.
Mrs P.:   Round. What's another word?
Child: Circle.
Mrs P.:   What shape are his legs?
Child: A tetrangle.

After questioning, some children are allowed to colour the puppet shapes on paper. Others must first finish their number work.

I ask Rashda to draw a picture of herself; of the teacher; and of me. A little reluctantly she does so, in approximately one minute per drawing. They are flattering to no one, but they do give sufficient information for Rashda to be assessed as slightly above average on the Goodenough—Harris *Draw-a-Man Test* (London: Harrap, 1963). This test requires the child to draw a man, a woman and herself. Each drawing is evaluated by totalling the number of items it shows, according to the check list (for example, head, eyes, nose, nostrils, ears, mouth, body, arms, hands, legs, feet). An average of the three scores gives the total score and this can then be reckoned against chronological age. Rashda's drawing of Mrs Parsons shows her with eight fingers, whereas the other two drawings reveal no fingers at all. Averaging out such items over three drawings permits account to be taken of bodily features which are only tentatively established in the child's mind.

Clearly, such a test can only be a rough guide to intelligence, since it omits any assessment of language, reasoning and number, and it has come in for severe criticism. In fact, its omissions are, in a sense, its strengths. In my view, its very simplicity and unusualness make it worth using and worth recording.

Having disposed of this diversion, Rashda returns to serious work and settles immediately to a green sum card, standing up as she works, and using her fingers to count, along with the dots on the paper. She achieves two correct answers and three reversals, as the following will indicate.

$$2 + 6 + 2 = 10$$

$$3 + 6 + 3 = 21$$

$$4 + 6 + 4 = 41$$

$$5 + 6 + 5 = 61$$

$$1 + 9 + 2 = 12$$

Class 8 is now fully occupied. Some children are colouring in parts of the geometric puppet, with a different colour for each separate shape; others are working on a variety of sum cards; others are queueing again by the teacher's desk to have their sums marked. The door is constantly opening and closing, as people come in and out. Mrs Parsons says, 'Because you're all using such great big voices, there'll be quiet for two whole minutes'. And there is.

Rashda finishes her sums and has them marked. Whether or not the fact of reversing the answers for sums two, three and four was pointed out to her is uncertain. She then collects her puppet shape for colouring. Some of the children have already decorated their puppets with buttons, eyes, eyebrows, noses, coats, etc., instead of merely colouring them in one uniform colour for each part. She begins by colouring the triangle hat in dark red, but then comes under the influence of the others and draws in some eyes, holding her picture up to me with the triumphant smile of an innovator.

As in the morning session, so now, children are constantly coming to make contact with me. 'Look! Look! they say, offering their work ... 'I live at 131' ... 'I live in another place' ... 'Do you count? asks Kuldip. When I nod, she commands me to count, which I do, up to twelve. Smiles and laughs from the group. Even these anthropologists use our numbers. I ask Rashda if she has a television at home. She nods her head.

R. M.: What programmes do you like?
Rashda: Dance.

It is now 2.15p.m. Rashda has copied Balwant's clown who was crying. In answer to the teacher's question regarding the crying, she explains, 'He's lost his mother'. Her own puppet drawing is now approved by Mrs Parsons and she is called for reading practice with the story *A Home in a Tree* (The McKee Platform Readers A3, by D. Castley, K. Fowler and S. Carstairs, London: Nelson).

Mrs Parsons points with her biro to one word at a time and Rashda pronounces most of them correctly, but whether she understands what she is reading is not certain. For example, the word *tall* occurred in the story and, when asked for the meaning of this word later, she replied *little*. Errors often tell us more than right responses. Such an error could be noted by Mrs Parsons in her reading records for subsequent attention, either by herself or by Mrs Matthews in an ESL session. Such liaison between staff is vital, and exchange of information can take place either outside teaching time or, when possible, by occasional observation of, and involvement in, each other's lessons.

Rashda's voice, incidentally, is much louder when reading than speaking. Up to this point it has been like Cordelia's in *King Lear*, 'soft, gentle and low'. While I am listening to her, one of the other girls tries to cut my hair with her scissors and smiles seraphically when I tell her I had it cut only the day before.

At 2.33p.m. Rashda has finished her reading of pages ten to thirteen, and is sitting on the floor cutting out her puppet. All around children are busily occupied in lawful or semi-lawful pursuits. One child is playing with some bricks; one with Lego; another croaking for fun. There is a group around the teacher with their cut-out puppets; a number sitting at tables colouring theirs; a few sitting on the floor cutting out their puppets; one mooing like a cow, or howling like a wolf, it is difficult to say which; three with a bowl of sand, playing happily.

This idyllic scene obtains for a few minutes until the teacher repeats the formula: 'Children!' She holds up her hands, the children follow suit, and there is silence in a second, which permits the clearing-up jobs to be distributed. All Class 8 move into action, hunting out scissors, crayons, bits and pieces of waste paper. It is obviously a popular activity and appears to be done very conscientiously. Rashda carries five tins of pencils. Mrs Parsons sets a time limit on the clearing up, and counts to five in order to speed the process: 'One...two...three...four...four and a half...four and three quarters...'

All except three or four children are now on the carpet and the corporate identity of the class is confirmed with a song in which they all participate. Perhaps it confirms their physical identity also, since it is one of those marvellous cumulative songs about parts of the body, which forces the children to concentrate very carefully as they perform actions appropriate to the words. For the non-English speakers, such relevant language repetition, of the kind that now follows, is excellent. It begins.

Mrs P.:   One finger, one thumb, one arm, one leg keeps moving,

When the song is over there is a momentary pause until the bell sounds and the children go out to play for fifteen minutes before returning at 3.05 p.m. for story time.

Mrs P.:   (*very gently*): I'm waiting to start the story and I don't want to have to wait for you...(*Pause.*) Once upon a time, there lived a king and a queen who were very happy. Except for one thing...

The children are again sitting on the mat in front of Mrs Parsons. Rashda occupies the same piece as earlier, sitting still, concentrating; now looking up at the teacher, now with her head on her folded arms. The story of *The Sleeping Beauty*, Ladybird version, continues.

Mrs P.:   They both longed to have children, but they had none. Every day they said to each other, 'If only we had a child.' Now, it happened one day, when the queen had been bathing, a frog crept out of the water and spoke to her. It said, 'Your wish shall come true. Before a year has gone by, you shall have a daughter.'

We are in the fantasy realm of kings and queens, magic wishes, and talking frog obstetricians.

Mrs P.:   (*showing a picture*): There's the frog, talking to the queen.

Child: Can frogs talk?

Mrs P.:   No. It's a magic frog.

          The queen was delighted and she hurried to tell her husband the good news.

Mrs Parsons reads well, with good stress and intonation, following the text very closely, with additional questions of her own about the pictures ('She looks wicked, doesn't she?') and about particular words:

Mrs P.:   She was furious. What does that mean?

Child: Ugly.

Child: Wicked.

Child: Angry.

Mrs P.:   Angry. Yes. Good girl. Angry.

One boy is playing with his teeth; another is picking his nose; a girl is doing her hair; two boys are sucking their fingers. But, despite these slight physical activities, all except one have their eyes firmly on the teacher and are concentrating on the story. Their attentiveness hardly wavers until, at 3.26p.m., 'They lived happily ever after'.

Coats and anoraks are collected, first by boys and then girls, as has been the sequence throughout the day.

Mrs P.:   Hands together and eyes closed.

The children do as asked, sitting cross-legged on the mat. Mrs Parsons sings one note and they all join in:

> Loving Father of the Children,
> I belong to you.
> Through the day-time
> And the night-time,
> You take care of me. Amen.

There is the same satisfying sensation of completeness at the end of the school day as occurred in Chapter 1 with Mike's experience.

We all now sit and wait for the bell, the children still cross-legged with arms folded, 'reaching up tall', as the phrase is. On the bell:

Mrs P.:   Goodnight, children.
Children: Goodnight, Mrs Parsons.
Mrs P.:   Say goodnight to Mr Mills.
Children: Goodnight, Mr Mills.
R. M.:   Goodnight, children.

Sequel 1 Teaching English to Bilingual Children

Methodology

English as a Second Language (ESL) teaching has gradually evolved its own pedagogic identity, according to its particular situation. However, it has always been influenced, to some extent, by the Teaching of English as a Foreign Language (EFL). Thus, for a time both favoured 'situational syllabuses', whereby grammatical structures were grouped around particular situations (for example, shopping; going to the park; road safety). This appears to be the kind of syllabus adopted by Mrs Matthews in Rashda's withdrawal group.

Those who were dissatisfied with this type of framework turned to what were called 'functional-notional syllabuses'. Here, language was grouped according to:

(1) functions (e.g. making requests; apologizing);
(2) notions (e.g. concepts of time, weight, measurement).

Subsequently, the discussion has moved on to methods rather than content, since even with a particular kind of syllabus, teachers may be emphasizing the *usage* of language rather than helping students to *use* it as and when they need to. Thus, among EFL practitioners, there has been much discussion about 'communicative' teaching. It has been felt that the more language could mirror real life, and the actual use students could put it to, the more effective it would be.

At the same time, primary school ESL was emerging from its dependence on previous EFL methods and reflecting a more child-centred approach, in keeping with the primary school ethos and curriculum. In this situation, the source of any syllabus comes to be the needs of particular children in a particular school, and the emphasis on 'using' language means that:

(1)   Activities have a real purpose (for example, children might make a game or a book for the rest of their class);

(2)   The content and purpose of language may be stressed more than the practice of particular structures (for example, children might perform a simple puppet play with repetitious language);

(3)   Authentic materials and situations will be used (e.g. children visit shops and buy ingredients for subsequent cooking activities);

(4)   There will be realistic practice (e.g. children use the social language for getting dressed after P.E.);

(5)   Teachers observe and listen to children, and each other, to discover what they actually say in different situations and what children need to say to operate socially and cognitively in school.

Part of the teacher's own monitoring of language will include, in the early stages, avoidance of slang (for example, 'Come on now, I'm only pulling your leg'). It will also include avoidance of rattling out a stream of instructions and exhortations, where a simple repeated phrase will be clearer. So there needs to be a precise understanding of what language (in terms of vocabulary and structures) will be used during any activity. Without this, the topic may be linguistically too broad and too varied, and the children will experience 'submersion' rather than 'immersion'.

Language Support

Mrs Matthews operates a withdrawal system from the classroom and this is by no means uncommon. Many other teachers prefer to work collaboratively within the classroom and this is reflected in the change in terminology from ESL teacher to Language Support Teacher.

It is argued that withdrawing children gives them the status of a 'problem' which, once removed from the classroom, is also removed from the class teacher's mind. In such circumstances, neither teacher can be really aware of what is happening in each other's area. They both need to integrate their activities and their language. Ideally, then, in a collaborative situation the classroom teacher can appreciate the linguistic demands made by the curriculum upon particular learners and the language support teacher can tailor the language to relevant curriculum work. Such a way of working demands organizational and interpersonal skills of a high order.

The Other Languages of England

One still encounters such comments as 'Don't use that language here, speak English' and 'He/she has no language'. Moreover, lack of English fluency may be equated with lack of intelligence. Associated with such views is the notion that use of the mother tongue is a disincentive to learning English and that over-generalization of rules between languages results in errors that impede further learning (known as 'first language interference').

However, a more positive attitude towards children's mother-tongue languages and errors in English has developed. Here, errors can be seen as inevitable and necessary, merely a stage (known as 'inter-language') which indicates the nature of the generalizations which the learner is making.

Moreover, the recognition that many children are developing bilingually once more reflects the child-centred bias of primary education. That is to say, teachers are looking more closely at what children bring to the learning situation. As far as schools are concerned, the benefits of such recognition are:

(1) One can build on the skills and talents which children bring to school and increase one's knowledge of individual boys and girls;

(2) Language diversity aids intellectual and cognitive development and the children have an opportunity to continue developing in their first language.

(3) Children's self-esteem and confidence are enhanced when they see that their home language is valued by the school;

(4) The links between the school and the local community can be strengthened and the resources of that community can enrich the life of the school;

(5) When community languages are given status by the school, this increases the language awareness of other children and helps to combat racism;

(6) Children have a more immediate access to the curriculum if concepts are explained in mother tongue.

The positive acceptance of bilingualism has resulted in new developments in schools. Three examples will suffice:

(1)   When teaching English, some teachers have worked on a bilingual methodology which obviates the need for Direct Method teaching by mono-lingual (English-speaking) teachers. Other teachers, classroom assistants, older students and outside agencies can work alongside the mono-lingual teacher as bilingual facilitators.

(2)   Some teachers have developed language awareness courses whereby languages (and, consequently, the languages and dialects which the children speak) are studied as a topic across curriculum areas such as history, geography, science and literature.

(3)   Some teachers positively promote and celebrate the development within the curriculum of children's home languages. Such promotion may range from mother-tongue story-telling sessions to collecting language items on audio tape from relatives, to putting up labels around the school in a variety of scripts.

As one 11-year-old child says, 'I speak Gujerati to my friends, I use English in the classroom, I read Urdu at Mosque, I learn the Koran in Arabic, and my mother speaks Marathi.'

Further Reading

Gregory, A. and Wollard, N. (1985) *Looking into Language Diversity in the Classroom* (Stoke-on-Trent: Trentham).

Houlton, D. (1984) *All Our Languages* (London: Edward Arnold).

Houlton, D. and Willey, R. (1983) *Supporting Children's Bilingualism* (Harlow, Essex: Longman).

Khan, V. (1985) *The Other Languages of England*: Linguistic Minorities Project (London: Routledge & Kegan Paul).

Open University P534 (1985) *Every Child's Language* (Milton Keynes: Open University).

Schools Council (1984) *Children's Language Project* (Andover: Philip & Tacey).

Tough, J. (1985) *Talk Two: Children Using English as a Second Language* (London: Onyx).

Sequel 2 Real Reading

More schools than ever are actively promoting strong links with the parents of their children and the community served by the school. Not only in the traditional areas of Parent-Teacher fund-raising and social activities but also in significant areas of the curriculum. For example, here is an extract from a booklet for parents (Waterland, 1985), reproduced by kind permission, designed to encourage and sustain parents in the partnership of developing children's reading habits, skills and enjoyment. The extract is not intended as a blueprint for others, since each school must design its own communications for parents, depending on particular circumstances and context.

The Printed Books

We do not use a reading scheme in the school; your child will not have 'flash cards', 'word tins' or pre-readers; nor will s/he have to work through Book 1, Book 2 and so on.

Instead, we have chosen a very wide range of 'real' story books – just the ones that you will find in the library or bookshop. They have been picked because they are good stories easy to read and remember, with predictable, natural language. These are the sort of books that children love to listen to and soon try to read for themselves.

"a highly prized library...."

If you want to buy or borrow books for your child, please do not go for 'reading schemes'; we, or your local librarian, will gladly recommend books your child will enjoy. A book club, the

See-Saw Club, is run by the school to help your choice and once a month your child will bring home an order form for a wide selection of very reasonably priced books. One book a month will grow into a highly-prized library which will do more than anything else to make your child feel like a real reader. His or her own library ticket is also a great boost.

SENTENCE MAKER BOOKS

As well as printed books your child will soon be making his or her own story books using a sentence maker. When these little books are finished they will be brought home to keep. Your child will enjoy reading them to you!

If you would like to see sentence maker being used by the children, please ask you child's teacher for an invitation to spend a morning in school so that you can see how these little books are made.

What can you do to help?

AT THE BEGINNING

Your child will bring home a 'book bag'. This will contain a book that your child has chosen and, at the back of the book, some notes for you suggesting approaches to the story.

It is *not* intended that you should teach your child to read this book; we do not expect him or her to come back to school able to read every word.

Instead, we hope that you will read the story with your child on your lap just as you always do but bearing in mind these points.

- Make sure the child can see the print and pictures.
- Point to the words as you read them.
- Use the pictures as well. There is often additional story in them.
- Allow plenty of time for discussion before you turn over. A valuable question is 'What do you think will happen next?'.
- Let your child 'read' the story to you afterwards – even if this is reciting by heart or making the story up from the pictures.

This is a very important stage. Children learn to behave like readers by these activities. Praise all their attempts.

If your child is too tired or reluctant to join in, just make it an opportunity for you to read in a relaxed, enjoyable way. Do not force participation.

When you and your child would like a different book send the book bag back to school for a 'refill'.

If your child particularly likes a story s/he may want to hear it over and over. This should be encouraged (if you can stand it!). You may find that a very well-loved story like this is the first one that your child learns how to read independently.

While you are undertaking these activities at home your child's teacher is doing just the same thing in the classroom. You and she are giving the children the very great experience of meaningful print that will move them nearer and nearer to being readers themselves.

"....bringing home a book bag...."

LATER ON

After your child has had a lot of books read to him or her and has gained many words in sentence maker work, you may find that his or her behaviour begins to change during story sessions. Now you will find your child beginning to pick out words in the book, reciting the text accurately and trying to match the spoken words with the text by pointing with a finger.

At this point, as you settle for a book session, ask the child, 'Shall I read or shall you?'. If the child would like to try then let him or her do as much as possible, being ready to help if your child asks you to.

Remembering these points will help.

71

- *Read the story to the child first.* This is not 'cheating', it is helping him or her to know where the story is going and helps prediction of the text.
- *Do not help and correct* when the child tries unless the child gets into real difficulties and has obviously lost the sense. Keeping quiet is difficult but children need to learn to puzzle out text from the sense they expect to find.
- *Do not worry if the child's reading is not word perfect.* If s/he is making sense it does not matter if s/he reads 'house' instead of 'home' or 'Good dog, Spot' instead of 'Good boy, Spot'.

It *would* matter, however, if s/he read 'he got on his house and rode away'. Obviously the sense has been lost and you should offer to take over if your child doesn't want to carry on or if s/he asks you to. Never make him or her feel that s/he *must* read. This destroys confidence and introduces the idea of testing and failure. Always be ready to read the story yourself if necessary.

At this stage it is helpful to see your child as beginning an apprenticeship in reading. S/he is going to work alongside you, the skilled craftsman; gradually the apprentice can undertake more and more of the task but you will continue to support and guide for as long as you both feel it is necessary.

LATER STILL

As your child's confidence and skill grows you will find s/he reading to you more and more. Bear in mind though that the children have free choice of books and may sometimes choose a book that they cannot yet manage alone. When this happens by all means return to the earlier activities and read to your child. S/he will still need to hear more difficult text than s/he can manage alone.

Remember also all the points on previous pages. It is vital that your child is confident, relaxed and sure s/he can make sense of the story. Don't apply pressure and don't insist on absolute accuracy. *The sense is the vital consideration.*

"....a book they cannot yet manage alone...."

Sequel 3 Teacher Training Tasks

Chapter 2 Rashda

(1) Do you share my views on the possible values of Rashda's school assembly? How might the 'hidden curriculum' be operating in the second hymn? Have you any reservations about assemblies in this kind of context? (See the Sequel on School Assemblies).

(2) What strategies are used throughout the day for getting the children's attention? What methods do you use? In what circumstances is it very difficult to be successful, no matter what your methods are?

(3) Does the classroom environment and equipment appear to you to be adequate? What do you consider an ideal classroom environment? Why?

(4) Discuss and/or produce materials and ideas for any of the following stimuli for encouraging and developing spoken language with young children:

    (a) Various displays: objects worthy of close examination; objects differing in colour, texture, smell, sound; natural phenomena; objects related to a particular theme, such as Earth, Air, Fire, Water.

    (b) Children's own collections: models; dolls/puppets; stamps; coins; pop-star pictures; fashion photos; football programmes; soldiers; precious objects; matchbox/dinky toys.

    (c) Hobbies and sports.

    (d) Clothes box.

    (e) Telephone.

    (f) Shops and shopping.

    (g) Sound effects.

    (h) Photographs, pictures, posters, drawings, cartoon strips.

    (i) Pets.

    (j) Play houses.

(k) Cooking.
(l) Objects from home which have a story.
(m) Books, newspapers, comics, magazines.
(n) Television, radio, films, video, computer, tape recorder.
(o) Visits outside and visitors into school.
(p) Local people in the community and members of the family.

(5) Discuss the lesson of English as a Second Language (ESL) in the light of the Sequel 'Teaching English to Bilingual Children'. Is this the kind of provision you would make for your boys and girls who have such needs?

(6) What do you feel about the 'magic carpet' ritual? Describe other rituals you have met.

(7) Discuss the apparent strengths and weaknesses of the small group reading lesson with Mrs Renshaw and devise an adequate record card by which to monitor Rashda's progress in reading.

(8) Look carefully at the extract from Northborough School's booklet to parents in the Sequel on 'Real Reading'. How would it need to be changed to fit your school or a school you know well? What are its messages about the nature of reading? In what ways is the extract 'user-friendly?' How might you react to it as a parent?

Chapter 3

David, Aged 7

When there's a fire they ring the bell,
like a bell when you go into school

The School

David's Church of England school was built in 1961 in the middle of an industrial city, and is surrounded by small factories – plastics, autocrome, press work. It has some 144 children and there is a nursery unit, a junior school and a comprehensive school, all in close proximity. The infants school is multi-ethnic, with more children of West Indian origin (30 per cent in David's class) than Indian or Pakistani, but a predominant number of white children.

David himself is first pointed out to me in assembly. He is well dressed in new, smart, patterned long trousers, a grey shirt, green pullover, brown shoes, blue socks. He has longish mousey hair and is taller than those around him, being a term or so older. His class teacher says that he was very unsure of himself when he first arrived from Yorkshire two terms previously, that he was slightly aggressive and ready to burst into tears at a moment. Miss Bennett felt that his attitude had improved enormously since that time.

The Day

Outside is a dull, rainy, gloomy day. Inside the large, light school hall there is a warm atmosphere as the headmistress, a well-dressed, smiling person with greying hair, welcomes two visitors to the assembly, the local Anglican curate and myself. The hall is set out with children grouped in rows around the central open square, and teachers at strategic intervals.

Mrs Manders, the headteacher, immediately involves different children in the assembly. First of all, several individuals display certain objects they have brought into school, such as books and dolls. A 'birthday boy' has brought a tin of Kit-e-Kat which he donates to Mrs Manders. John has an announcement regarding the stamp club; it will meet the next day in the afternoon. Such clubs (as stamp, chess, drama, music, model making, art) operate in many a primary school on one afternoon a week. They give the children opportunity to get to know a wider range of children than merely those in their own class.

After such individual activity there is corporate involvement with a sung prayer, the children's own silent prayer, and then hand gestures appropriate to gramophone music, that is, first swaying like branches in the wind, then rain-like movements. David looks carefully at what others are doing and joins in tentatively for a second or so every now and again. He is obviously unused to this activity. When the music is finished it is named, by the children, as *Aquarium* and there are a few questions about the nature and appearance of an aquarium. No such opportunity for a widening of vocabulary would be missed by any experienced teacher.

Then the curate tells his story:

There was once a magic pair of boots and each boot believed itself to be the shinier of the two. They didn't realize that they were going to have to live together all their lives. A soldier bought them and went on guard at the Tower of London, dressed in a very smart red and gold uniform and a new pair of black boots. The left boot didn't like the fact that the right boot was always told to go first when they started marching and it leaned across and tied the laces together. The soldier fell flat on his nose. (*Laughs from the children.*) The soldier was very annoyed and told his boots how naughty they were. But the boots merely tried to outdo each other for speed and the soldier went faster than all the other soldiers. The right boot was jealous that the left boot was overtaking him and the left boot complained that the right one had hit him when the Commanding Officer called 'Attention!' and all the soldiers were meant to click their heels together. So an argument started between the two boots and they were fighting each other, just like children having a quarrel in the playground. The soldier was in trouble now and all because the boots hadn't learnt to get on with each other; not to be jealous of each other; not to stop saying 'me first'. At the end of the day the soldier sold the boots and the shopkeeper put them on the second-hand shelf. And if you invite me back again, I'll tell you if anyone else bought the boots.

The curate has told the story with good humour and an easy manner, at an appropriate speed and with much eye contact. He has used mime, where relevant, to illuminate his words and thus cater for a wide range of listener, and he has interspersed a number of questions to which the children readily responded. There was an excellent atmosphere and the children, sitting cross-legged on the floor, were silent and attentive. None more so than David, who followed each turn in the narrative as carefully as if he had been a foreigner in a strange country listening to directions. There is marvellous power in a good story well told, and the curate has taken care not to kill it by over-stressing the moral element.

Moreover, it is good for children to have regular contact with adults from the local community outside the school walls. The 1944 Education Act recognized the local education authority's responsibility to contribute to the 'spiritual, mental and physical development of the community' and such responsibility is mutual and cyclical. Indeed, the 1988 Education Reform Bill seeks to strengthen the role of parents, through their elected representatives on governing bodies, to have a say in the implementation of the national curriculum and in the matter of local financial management and control.

The assembly continues and we now witness the full ritual accorded a birthday boy or girl. The birthday boy mentioned earlier had had his celebration at a previous assembly. Now it is the turn of James, who has brought a packet of birthday cards to show the children. These are held up one by one and Mrs Manders says something about each. The children laugh as they see pictures of long-trunked elephants and furry tigers, and then all join in the sung greeting: 'We wish you many happy returns of the day, James.' Everyone counts as seven candles are lit in the middle of the hall. Another song. Seven claps by everyone in the hall, and then single staccato claps as James blows out his candles one by one. It is a highly effective ceremony, which has delighted James, gripped all onlookers, and marked the end of assembly.

The message of the ritual is clear. In this brief moment in the school year, the whole community downs tools to acknowledge James's existence. He and, by implication, every other individual has significance within this group of people. He is made to feel important and valued. Next day, or next week, will be someone else's turn. As you will see at the end of this chapter, David acknowledges that he has not yet felt able to face this public expression of belonging. That, in itself, is significant.

The children stand, class by class, clapping to the accordion music on the gramophone, and depart leaving a class behind which contains David. He has been highly involved throughout the proceedings and adapted well to the change in rhythm of the various claps.

It is 9.40a.m. and David's class awaits their movement lesson. One girl approaches and asks me to write 'Beverley number 20'. When this is done she points it out to a group of her friends. It seems to be part of a testing-out process which some young children employ with a stranger. Evidently this one can write; he might be useful to me. David tells me he lives in the fire station and his number is 14. I assume, wrongly, from this that he is a fairly confident boy, since I have not yet spoken to him and he does not know that I am to spend the day monitoring his activities. Another boy tells me that his father is the school caretaker. Yet another is the local vicar's son. These isolated introductions have been made while the rest of the class was preparing for the register.

All now sit at the teacher's feet while names are checked, girls first. Miss Bennett, who has been Class 4's teacher for three weeks, accomplishes the task quietly and efficiently. She is a teacher of Welsh origin and one year's experience, being in her early 20s. She has recently been ill, and for anyone feeling even slightly unwell teaching is miserably remorseless. She tells the children that there are only five minutes left for them in the hall and they are to take off their shoes and socks. David does this very quickly and lines up with the others, all carrying shoes, socks, pullovers, which are deposited in a long line at the side of the hall.

Each child now finds a space and moves about the hall to the noise of the tambourine as 'wibbly wobbly jellies'. They 'reach up tall' on tiptoe several times. They run round the hall, weaving in and out without touching anyone. 'Use your mind', says Miss Bennett, 'come on, Andrew, you're being silly.' They run to the sound of the tambourine; they stamp 'like great heavy giants, very slowly'. Now they shout STAMP! as they stamp, and they laugh when they stop in the middle of the word 'st ... ' They are exhorted to move with 'twirling and twisting tiny quiet feet, like the snowflakes yesterday', and they do so. Then they race round the hall to the noise of the tambourine and prove the unwritten law that, in such a situation, children always move anticlockwise, as any teacher knows. One boy, Dean, is sent to stand by the door for sliding. Finally, as a winding-down exercise, they go round 'like trotting horses with knees up high', as the teacher taps out the rhythm on a piece of wood.

The potential of this kind of range of physical responses is clearly recognised and endorsed in official circles, as a Department of Education and Science document indicates. *The Curriculum from 5 to 15* (1985) states:

Schools should provide opportunities for vigorous physical activity through adventure play and for bold movement and increasingly fine control through the use of large and small equipment. In addition, children should engage in expressive movement in response to stimuli such as music and stories.

There is also a view that physical education may be especially of value to many children retarded in their reading and writing. The theory is that the fine physical and visual control needed for handwriting and reading can develop from a refinement of large, crude movements in PE and drawings in art which precede it. This is akin to the kind of progress a baby makes in the third year of life, when she or he can unscrew bottle tops, manipulate 'Lego' materials, hammer a small peg with accuracy and control. Such thinking has underpinned the development by A. E. Tansley of a screening device for identification of clumsy children in need of special help (see Lambert, 1976).

Having had practice, then, in the co-ordination of movement and sound, experienced a variety of rhythms, and possibly developed their language a little, as well as enjoyed themselves, the children line up in the middle of the hall, without a sound, and collect their bundles of clothes, like refugees, before standing by the door, boys and girls in separate ranks.

The importance of an understood and ordered routine in much of what goes on in school would be accepted by most teachers. This is not an argument for mindless regimentation. Quite the reverse. Good organization and management is a prerequisite for innovation and there should certainly be opportunities throughout any school week for children to exercise initiative and learn how to manage freedom and choice. However, in PE a precise framework is an essential in its own right, as a condition of health and safety. To organise a good PE lesson, so that all children operate enjoyably in safety and with new tasks, is one of the most demanding challenges a student teacher can face.

The children now make the short walk down the corridor to the classroom, David being last in line and closing the door. It is 10.05 a.m. and the children sit very quietly on the floor, putting on shoes and socks. One of them is crying. 'Oh!, Conway, be brave', exhorts Miss Bennett and continues to issue rebukes, questions, advice, encouragement to individuals. David has pulled his lace out of one shoe and a girl, quite unsolicited, comes to his aid and threads it for him. He later pulls the laces out again, for Miss Bennett to re-thread them. Perhaps he feels it is a job for experts, or perhaps it is one of his ploys for gaining adult attention.

A question and answer session now develops as they continue to dress themselves. Miss Bennett, who is lacing another pair of shoes on her lap, says that so far they have only two items for their class news book – a picture of a hamster called Tich, and Beverley's story about King Kong. What other news can they add? Contributions are offered with the confidence of hesitant salesmen unconvinced of the value of their product. Nicola watched Donald Duck and Mickey Mouse television cartoons with her Mum and Dad, Grandad and Grandma. Neil merely 'watched tele'. Julie went to the doctor with her mother and then watched television but, like Neil, cannot remember the programme. The teacher asks Brian if he played with his brothers and sisters, but this elicits no response. He only reacts when television is mentioned and he speaks of Woody Woodpecker. Lynn tidied up her toys but is informed by Miss Bennett that 'that is not very interesting'. Hugh says he helped Elizabeth to make Louise's bed and then they played with a very small dolly, catching it on the back of their hands. David sits on his knees at the back, saying nothing. Sharon tells the world that her mother is going into hospital to have a baby.

Miss B.: But I saw your mother this morning. When's the baby going to arrive?
Sharon: I dunno, I ain't seen it yet.
Miss B.: And where's it going to come from?
Sharon: I dunno.
Child: Out of Mummy's tummy.

Such an open forum for children's news is a common occurrence in infant and junior schools and, provided that each item, however trivial apparently, is accepted and used as a growth point from which a little more discussion may stem, then it can be a very valuable activity indeed. At best, it relates the worlds of home and school; it convinces the children that their experience matters and is worth talking about; it gives them the opportunity to get a better grip on that experience by putting it into words.

At 10.17 a.m. the children move into seven groups all round the room. There are twenty-one boys and thirteen girls and the tables are loosely ordered in terms of ability, David's group being the slowest. In this way, non-streaming within the basic structure of the school's organisation becomes streaming within the confines of the classroom, as the 1978 HMI survey, *Primary Education in England*, pointed out.

The room is very attractive and, amongst other items, contains notices which give it a domestic warmth, such as:

> SHARON'S PATTERN REMINDS HER OF CHRISTMAS

> CONWAY SAW SOME WEDDING TAXIS IN THE STREET

> HARDEEP LIVES IN THIS RED HOUSE

> CAN YOU SEE THE BUDS OPENING INTO LEAVES?

> ROBIN HOOD IS FIGHTING PRINCE JOHN

Such notices as these, drawing as they do on children's own experience, comments and interests, can serve as a prelude to

the development of individual books or folders of personal news
or information.

There is a star chart on the partition and all Class 4 children
have been awarded stars except Neil, Dean, Beverley, Donna,
Conway, Hardeep and David. Ridgway (1976) urges caution in
the use of such external rewards and incentives. She writes: 'A
child's self-esteem is very dependent on the view the teacher
takes of him: the response of the teacher to what he does is
often interpreted by him as an assessment of his own value ...
Star and no-star may be interpreted by children as "I'm good and
he's bad".' Certainly, praise and rebuke may be received by many
children as moral judgements upon them, and a school, like no
other institution, issues both with the profligacy of a busy machine
gun. As Philip Jackson (1968) observes: 'Schools are places in which
rewards and punishments are administered in abundance. Smiles,
compliments, special privileges, good grades, and high scores on
tests are occasioned by certain kinds of classroom behaviour.
Frowns, scoldings, deprivations, poor grades, and low scores on
tests are occasioned by other kinds.'

Books and materials are ready on each set of tables, and
tasks are distributed, group by group. One is to copy sums from
the blackboard; another to do some writing; another, including
David, to match words (on yellow cards) with pictures (also on
yellow cards). His partner, Stacey, first announces: 'Look at me. I've
got a star', and then adopts a more altruistic stance by showing
David the cards.

David: What's the word?
Stacey: *Kuh ... a ... ruh. (This is no help to David and he asks
          the teacher.)*
David: *Kuh.*
Miss B.: What do the next two letters say? (*No response.*)
          aah ...
          What do *kuh* and *aaah* say?
David: Car.

Success at last, but, having matched the word with a picture of
a car, he is uncertain as to his next move and watches Beverley,
who is drawing a picture of a clown.

Meanwhile, Miss Bennett issues a stream of comments as she
moves from group to group round the room: 'Come on, Sharon

... All right, Maxine? ... Stephanie's nearly finished ... Go and fetch some crayons, Beverley ... Shush, Julie, you don't have to talk about it.' 'Miss', says Stacey, 'I ain't gorra horinge'.

It is 10.30 a.m. and David is laboriously copying 'Wednesday' from the blackboard. His task is made more difficult in that he has his back to the board and turns round, not merely for each letter, but for each part of a letter. Moreover, he does not concentrate on what he is doing but looks first at Stacey's book, then Beverley's. His final version is:

we dNeday

No labour of Hercules caused more problems. David is in the early stages of getting to grips with the complexities of writing and may still need much practice at a more elementary level. A sequence of writing development activities as that which I will now outline would be, broadly speaking, acceptable to many teachers and, for further detail, Chapter 2 of Gloyn and Frobisher (1975) may be consulted. The points are numbered one to twelve for convenience since there would often be no clear dividing line between them. Each child would need to dovetail into the sequence as and where appropriate.

(1)   Opportunity for play with manipulative toys and materials, e.g. 'Lego', jigsaws, Plasticine.
(2)   Opportunity to make pictures with a variety of materials in addition to paint, e.g. leaves, bottle tops, wood shavings, wool.
(3)   Colouring in of simple shapes and pictures, using crayon or pencil.
(4)   Tracing of shapes and letter patterns of increasing sophistication, followed by free drawing of these patterns and, later, proper letter formation.
(5)   Copying of own name in large letters. Later, this from memory.

(6) Close copying on top of (and later underneath) teacher's writing, accompanied by appropriate and attractive decoration of the page.
(7) Constant and on-going discussion of activities and content.
(8) Written captions for child's own paintings or pictures.
(9) Class and/or individual news book, based on children's real experience.
(10) Close copy of teacher's writing, eventually followed by close copy of material from work card and, later, far copy from blackboard.
(11) Development and use of word banks, whether in shoe pockets, 'Breakthrough to Literacy'-type folders or, later, notebooks arranged in alphabetical order.
(12) Free writing, based on child's own activities, model, drawings, etc., with increasing sophistication of style.

Certain schools participating in, or endorsing the aims of, the National Writing Project (School Curriculum Development Committee, 1985–88) would put stress on children's invented spelling and writing, if it helps them see themselves as 'real' writers; on drafting and re-drafting; on writing, where possible, for a real audience and for a range of purposes.

David has now realized that he can copy the date, 29 January, more easily from Stacey than from the blackboard and this he does before wrestling with drawing and writing.

Miss B.: Come on David, it's taking you a long time.
David: (*to Stacey, twice*): Do you have to do it in pencil or crayon?

Like many a diffident child, he is afraid of making mistakes. Receiving no answer, he tries Miss Bennett.

Miss B.: What do we usually do our pictures with?
David: Crayons.

He now chooses a purple crayon to draw his car. He is the only one still working at his table. Suddenly he looks at my notebook and says, 'You've done two Davids'. It is true enough, but if he really has recognized the words from my scrawl, then he possesses talent far beyond what is apparent. He asks me why I write like that (presumably he means scribble) and, when I tell him it is quicker, it reminds me that there is no very good reason why he should be forced to work at an unnatural pace. He is neither lazy nor naughty. Merely slow.

Miss B.:   Have you finished, David?
David: No. (*Shakes his head.*)
Miss B.:   Hurry up.

The rest of the children collect their coats one by one and line up by the door before going out to play. On his way, Brian tells me, 'All that writing is yours, isn't it?' and, by this simple means, makes the brief human contact he needs.

Only David and I are left in the classroom. He is standing at the front of the room, sucking his drink through a straw; I am finishing my notes before coffee in the staff room. Outside in the corridor Miss Bennett may be heard organizing children.

At 11.00 a.m. break is over and a group is extracted from the class for special remedial attention. Such a withdrawal policy can be an effective way of coping with individual weaknesses (and strengths) as was seen in Chapter 2. In order to work successfully, the withdrawal time from normal classes should not be excessive; the composition of the groups should change to meet differing needs; and, above all, the attitude to the system itself should be right. On one occasion, in another school not discussed in this book, as weak readers were going out of the classroom to their separate lesson, I heard a remaining pupil comment, 'The mentals are off'.

The nine extracted children here, including David, go to a brightly decorated and attractive classroom which has a variety of pieces of equipment strategically spaced about. In this room Mrs Wilder, a smartly dressed dark, clearly spoken teacher of considerable experience, provides intensive work throughout the day for group after group.

She begins today's session by organizing the children in a semi-circle on the floor in front of her. Then she tosses cardboard shapes down on the floor and the children call out the correct name – oblong, square, circle, triangle. At one point Derek says painfully, 'Oh! God, I've forgotten it'. A moment later Mrs Wilder asks David the difference between [⎯⎯⎯⎯⎯⎯] and ☐ .

Pointing to the oblong, he says, 'It's got two little sides and two big sides'.

There is an excellent atmosphere and work proceeds at a steady pace, underpinned by unobtrusive yet clear discipline. The teacher is kind and quietly spoken and accepting. Above all, she has planned the work carefully, knows precisely what she is doing, and the children inevitably fall under the spell of the clear framework for activity. They are to attempt tasks appropriate for their ability and interests. Here, then, are at least eight ingredients which, when skilfully combined, could hardly fail to produce a successful lesson.

Mrs Wilder shows the group a card on which are printed three shapes, as shown in Figure 3.1.

Figure 3.1

Stacey has the opportunity to match single cardboard shapes on the floor with those on the card. She manages the triangles but tries to superimpose a square on top of the rectangle. New boy Brian now tries the card shown in Figure 3.2.

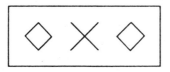

Figure 3.2

When he succeeds, the children 'give him a big clap'. The approval of one's peers is a powerful incentive.

David attempts the card shown in Figure 3.3.

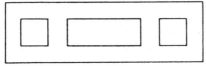

Figure 3.3

He is rewarded, like Brian, by applause when he succeeds. By such means the sense of corporate identity and desire for group success is strengthened. He now tries another (Figure 3.4), with words of encouragement from Derek, 'Think very hard, David'.

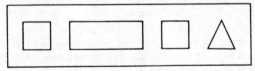

Figure 3.4

But he fails to remember the triangle at the end.

The activity, which is very popular, continues for another minute or so, punctuated by constant and genuine advice from dominant Derek, who is very proud of his own attainments in this area and, like all of us, needs to be successful in something.

After this practise of visual discrimination, which is also a pre-reading and pre-writing activity, Mrs Wilder moves to tactile experience, and tosses on to the floor small blue cards which have different pieces of material pasted to them. In threes, the children are told to feel them. Derek says, 'This one is much softer and this is a little bit rough'. In this way, the tactile discrimination finds expression in language which, as the activity progresses, should be of increasing refinement. Virtually everything that happens in school is capable of being used as a language opportunity.

The children attempt to test what they have experienced and Beverley is the first to stand up, feel a texture behind her back, without seeing it, and then attempt to locate that same texture on one of the blue cards in front of her on the floor. She succeeds first time and earns a clap. David tries but, although close, is not quite right. Only the teacher knows which is correct, as each child has a turn.

At 11.16a.m. the activity changes to sound discrimination. Mrs Wilder calls out some words – *catch cat cot pot can* – and the children try to spot the odd one out. Brian thinks *cot*; James *pot*; David *catch*; Derek *pot*.

Mrs W.:	Why are Derek and James right?
Derek:	Because it's got a *p*.
Mrs W.:	Try this one: *dog den hen dad dig*.

Beverley and Brian plump for *dig*; Derek and James, drunk with their previous success, incautiously vote for *dad*; Mandy and David settle for *hen*.

After four minutes several rounds of this new game have been played and it is time for pair work. Two children use the Bell & Howell Language Master machine; two are completing unfinished shapes. Two are joining dots to follow a pattern. Stacey and David work together with two cards of shapes. They have to repeat the sequence of shapes on the paper, which is so constituted that anything drawn may be easily erased.

When David has completed his card he reads the shapes to the teacher; gets them all correct; rubs them out and returns to his seat for the next exercise, which involves visual discrimination of a more subtle kind. He has a chart on which he will ring repeats of words found in the left-hand column.

David counts the words in my notebook as I have been copying the chart – seven – and checks them with his own, which he has all correct. In answer to his question, I tell him I have finished the card and he takes it off for checking. He has, in fact been very solicitous for my welfare all morning, seeing to it that I have a chair, opening the door, checking my work, and so on. Such consideration for others is rarely as noticed or rewarded in schools as academic success.

There is now a hint of trouble as Beverley says, 'That boy's putting his tongue out at me'. In some circumstances such a statement could be easily glossed over, but Beverley, so I was told later, is prone to work herself into a frenzy at the slightest provocation and will then spend up to an hour rocking herself to and fro, a clear indication of disturbance. Mrs Wilder takes her on her lap and cuddles her back into a good mood, while two of the boys look on sympathetically. It is as natural an act within the context of the lesson as asking a question, and it succeeds in solving the problem before it has really had time to develop.

Mrs Wilder's treatment of Derek is similarly skilful. He is known as a volatile child, who will react with violent aggression at any hint of criticism from another child, such as 'You've got it wrong'. With praise and encouragement he is a delightful person, co-operative, warm, and good humoured. He now says, 'Miss, I'm getting too clever'. 'Yes, you're getting too clever for me', replies Mrs Wilder, without a trace of irony, and his self-image receives a welcome boost.

Beverley and Derek are merely two of the nine who have obvious personality problems. In fact, each of the nine seems to have some degree of disturbance, but is skilfully contained within the security of this lesson and the warmth of the relationship. I was told later that 30 per cent of the children in David's class come from broken homes, and it is information for reflection rather than immediate action. What should a teacher do about such knowledge, when the simple stereotype of 'the broken home' may be as dangerous as that of 'The West Indian child' or 'The underachiever'? Perhaps the key point is that while relevant background knowledge about a child's domestic situation, family relationships, attitudes, interests, health, and so on, helps to make that child more of a real person in the eyes of the teacher, it will not lead instantly to the panacea of a perfect teaching programme. However, it must, in some way, inform the entire educational experience, and assist in the process of turning teaching fodder into whole persons, with independent integrity. With such thoughts in mind, some words of A. S. Neill (1939) have even more force than usual. He writes: 'A good teacher does not draw out; he gives out, and what he gives out is love. And by love I mean approval, or, if you like, friendliness, good nature. The good teacher not only understands the child, he approves of him.' There is no sentimentality here, for the 'love' finds expression in professional concern and expertise. And, no doubt, Neill meant to refer to both men and women.

Meanwhile, two of the recipients of this concern and expertise, David and Stacey, have moved to the Language Master corner and they begin their work here with a question and answer session designed to clarify certain preposition problems. David shows Stacey a card which has on it a picture of some children jumping above a box. Stacey says that the key word is *under*; the card number is matched with the mark card and her answer is seen to be incorrect. She puts a cross by number six; the original picture card is fed through the Language Master and the word *above* is spoken by the machine. This process is repeated seven times with other cards designed to teach the words *under* and *above*. Stacey gets seven out of eight correct, retaining the correct ones, and her card records her success.

Having finished this, the two children take the card to the teacher. Stacey, skipping her way there and looking very pleased with herself, says, 'Miss, I only got one wrong'. When their work is marked they return to the machine, taking a quick glance at the play house *en route*, and change chairs. They now reverse tasks and Stacey asks the questions. When David answers correctly she comments, in the role and language of teacher, 'That's a good boy', unwittingly investing academic success with a moral dimension. When David sees card number six of the children jumping above the box he says, 'jumping', for which he gets a cross since the word spoken by the machine is *above*. I tell him he was right, in a way, but both children are, not surprisingly, rather baffled. When they have their work checked I notice that he explains about *jumping*. Mrs Wilder spots that his two incorrect answers should both have read *above*, and she notes down this information in her records, no doubt for next time.

David and Stacey now move to their last activity of the morning, which is to transfer different coloured shapes on one piece of squared paper to another piece of squared paper. It is a matching exercise involving shape, colour and location.

He begins with purple, counting carefully across the centi-metre-squared paper to find the correct location. He tells Stacey that hers is wrong (which is true) and that his brother is called 'Chatterbox'. The two facts do not appear to be significantly related. However, if Stacey is in difficulty, then so is David, particularly with the colours, although that is not all. He realizes that the green shape is wrong (he started one square too high) but he continues on brown without making any attempt to correct his original error. I know, from having tried it, just how much care and co-ordination the exercise involves, and it is interesting that David did not try to correct the error he had made. The acceptance of such error seems to imply a kind of fatality. Either that, or a lack of concern, and this would seem to be uncharacteristic.

However, he is saved from further exertions as time is running out and the children are told to write their names on their papers so that the exercise may be finished the next day. And that is, apparently, that, when Mark tells the teacher that there is a dead man in the play house. My immediate reaction, rather a callous one, is to speculate on this as the theme for a television play. Who is the dead man? How did he get there? How should he appear to a child looking in through the play house window? How do the children react when they see the body? Such clinical and hard-hearted reflections are ended by the sober truth. Mrs Wilder, who has clearly encountered many such dead bodies in her time, takes us all to inspect the corpse. But, peer as we may through the door and windows, not one dead man can we see. Nor even a dead fly. I must confess to a mild degree of disappointment. Even so, that play house was never quite the same for me, and perhaps the children, too, endowed it with some peculiarly dramatic quality thereafter.

The incident provides a rather macabre ending to an otherwise normal sequence of events. It should not draw attention away from the high-quality teaching which these children have experienced over the past hour. In general terms, they have had teaching and reinforcement in the basic skill areas of shape, texture, sound and word recognition and discrimination, as well as development of the senses of sight, touch and hearing. All have experienced some success while engaged in a variety of interesting language and number activities in a secure atmosphere. (Even the prospect of a dead man shook no one's equanimity, except perhaps mine.) They have, at times, been responsible for their own progress, as well as being encouraged to co-operate together and develop important social skills. A good time has been had by all, and learning has undoubtedly been achieved.

It is now dinner time, but before we eat, David and I talk for a few minutes about his home (he says he has a dad and a brother) and interests. He lives in the local fire station and really comes alive in our discussion as he talks of the work his dad does.

R. M.: Now, David, did you tell me this morning that you lived in the fire station?

David: Yes.

R. M.: Is that right?

David: Yes.

R. M.: Tell me about that. What's it like living in a fire station?

David: When you first got there?

R. M.: Yes.

David: Me dad's working like a fireman. There's a big built tower. A man in it. When the fireman comes just pretends dead he's dead. There's smoke coming out of it. Then you get firemen get some hose on. They put water in it and the fire engine and the water comes out the pipe and ...

R. M.: Yes, go on.

David: ... and when there's a fire they ring the bell, like a bell

92

	when you go into school.
R. M.:	I know. And when the bell rings, what can you see from your window?
David:	When I'm playing out fire engine up at the firemen go up in the tower and they go really fast and or like cars in the way they move out the way, don't they, sometimes?
R. M.:	They do.
David:	And fire when er ... ambulance goes fast when somebody knocks some people over. They go really fast. Put the sirens on when they meet cars in the way they just go vroom!
R. M.:	It's exciting, being a fireman, isn't it?
David:	Yes.
R. M.:	What do you want to be when you grow up?
David:	A fireman.
R. M.:	Do you?
David:	A bird shooter.
R. M.:	A bird shooter?
David:	Yes.
R. M.:	Yes.
David:	A horse rider.
R. M.:	Horse rider, yes.
David:	And ... Indian.
R. M.:	And an Indian, yes.
David:	Cowboy.
R. M.:	Cowboy, yes.
David:	And erm ... ambulance man.
R. M.:	An ambulance man.
David:	And erm car driver.
R. M.:	A car driver.
David:	And er ...
R. M.:	Well, can you be all those things?
David:	Yes.
R. M.:	Can you? Heavens. That's a lot, isn't it? You're going to be very busy (*laughs*).
David:	Have to go whowhowho (*Indian yodelling noise*) ... tch! (*the sound of a cowboy gun firing*).

If asked to write about his father's job, it is doubtful if David could have produced more than a line or so. But the experience is there and shows itself, not only by what he says, but in the way he says it. He is more animated at this point than at any stage during the morning and his enthusiasm is indicated in the broken sentences, the onomatopoeic utterances, the clear if disjointed narrative sequence and, above all, the helter-skelter sensation of movement and excitement.

It is a useful strategy for a teacher occasionally to tape record the spoken words of a poor writer and transcribe them later, thereby giving him the satisfaction of having produced a piece of 'written work' which, in our educational system, is a form of higher status than spoken language. Given the opportunity, David would readily respond to the invitation to talk about his world. Apart from his obvious enthusiasm for the fireman's life, he has many other interests, witness his list of prospective occupations. Such experience will remain vague and shadowy unless given flesh in spoken language. There need to be constant opportunities in school for all children to talk about their experiences and interests and, thereby, get a better grip on them and on themselves. Perhaps, in the process, our notion of what constitutes a 'remedial' child will undergo radical modification. We are all remedial in some area.

However, now we move from one branch of the public services, the fire brigade, to another, the school meals sector, and an excellent lunch of hamburgers, parsnips, potatoes, Yorkshire pudding, cabbage, gravy, and chopped-up fresh fruit (that is, apples, bananas, oranges) with custard. All this punctuated by conversation between Samantha, Maria, Wayne, Hugh, David and myself about teeth, dentists and fillings. It began, as good conversations often do, with an observation drawn from real life, and one of the children commenting on the gold tooth which I have. Actually, it is a filling between two front teeth made of National Health gold. The conversation then continued with the children, at intervals, opening their mouths and stuffing fingers down throats, along with hamburger, to point out various natural and acquired phenomena, for my benefit. All very entertaining, but not for those of a queasy disposition. Teeth, accidents, animals, babies, being sick, seem to be topics of great interest to young children.

After dinner I return to the classroom, outwardly unscathed by the mealtime encounter, to prepare for the afternoon session. The door opens.

Child: (*shouting from the doorway*): Are you a doctor?

R. M.: No, dear, I'm not.

But the suggestion is reasonable and, to a child, it would make more sense than any true justification one could offer for such observation and note-making. Certainly, the children are rightly curious regarding my presence among them. When they come in at 1.30p.m., many of them sliding on their knees across the wooden floor, a number crowd around asking, 'What are you writing?' ... What are you doing? ... 'You're always writing, aren't you?' You may remember from Chapter 1 that Mike's 5-year-old contemporaries completely ignored their classroom intruder. By the age of 7, such insularity is less likely. It will reappear later, but for different reasons.

The children group themselves on the floor in front of Miss Bennett's desk. David is sitting in the same position as this morning, territorial stability being an important thing, as was noticed in Chapter 2. Silence falls and the teacher calls the register, girls first. Someone knocks at the door and a few of the children call out, 'Come in'. The visitor (the same Derek as appeared before lunch), enters but is turfed out immediately by Miss Bennett who explains, 'I'm the one who says "Come in"'. A few seconds later, to prove the point, she repeats the open sesame formula, 'Come in', and Derek re-enters to ask for the next of Mrs Wilder's groups. Three boys and a girl go off and the remainder of Class 4 moves into Neil's group, Mark's group, Julie's group.

It is customary in many schools to organize children in small groups, presumably so that a wider range of activities may be followed with only limited resources, or that it may be administratively convenient for the teacher. There is, too, the opportunity for more social learning to occur and for interaction between the group members.

Such an arrangement of the environment does promote easy communication and interchange of ideas but, on occasion, opportunities for co-operative work and mutual discussions are overlooked. The children may be physically grouped together, apparently for some corporate purpose, whereas, in reality, they are often pursuing solitary activities. In such a case, there may be little interaction between them. Close physical proximity does not lead automatically to all benefits.

Moreover, even where pupils are working corporately, is the quality of their interaction, and particularly their language, sufficient to justify the method of grouping? In this respect, Douglas Barnes asks some pertinent questions (1976) which are applicable across a wide age range. Here are four of them:

(1)   Are your pupils really discussing the meaning of what they are doing? For example, in science are they talking about how their 'experiment' relates to the principle in question, or is their talk mainly at the 'Pass the matches!' level?

(2)   Can they find problems and formulate them, put forward explanatory hypotheses, use evidence to evaluate alternatives, plan lines of action?

(3)   Can they cope with differences of opinion, share out the jobs to be done, move steadily through a series of tasks, summarize what they have decided, reflect on the nature of what they are doing?

(4)   Have the topics which they have chosen, or you have prescribed, led to useful discussions?

Clearly, such questions are important even, with a liberal degree of interpretation, at this 7-year-old stage. Clearly too, the teacher's level of language awareness must be high, if David's performance in a group is to be adequately monitored. The rough level of social skill may be immediately apparent – either by presence or absence – but to assess spoken utterance competently requires a finely attuned ear. This concept of 'appraisal' of children's language is interestingly explored by Joan Tough (1976) and, from a very different perspective, by Gordon Wells (1987).

Meanwhile, David, naturally oblivious to such consideration, returns to the picture and word exercise he was working on earlier in the morning.

Miss B.:   Come on David, or you'll be miles behind.
Beverley: (*to me*) Hello, I like you sitting next to us.
David: When we go somewhere, you go with us, don't you?
Beverley: Are you our group?
R. M.:   Yes, Beverley.
Beverley: (*to others*) He's our group.

David now writes CAR under his picture of a car. He had previously written CAT under it. This done, he finds a picture of an apple and a card with the single word APPLE on it, and settles down to draw the apple. He works slowly, humming to himself. His thought processes may be slow, but he is by no means unintelligent. Mandy and Beverley are moved by the teacher to other activities, but David tries another picture and single word. This time the picture is of a vase and he asks me if he has chosen the correct word; he is aware it begins with *vuh*. At the same moment, Beverley is drawing two boats and writing the number 2 on her paper; Stephen, three girls and the number 3; Mandy, eight stars with the number 8; Stacey, three flowers and the number 3. David asks himself: 'I've finished that, what shall I do next?' Undecided, he turns to Beverley.

David: How many do you have to do on these?
Beverley: Fifty, sixty, seventy.

Then, having advised him extravagantly, she counts out some other cards for him and asks, 'Have you done that one?' David again voices his thoughts aloud: 'I don't know how to do ships. I'll have a try.' He does so.

It is now 2.00p.m. and twelve children are still working at their tables while the rest are grouped on the floor around the teacher with their 'Janet and John' reading books. After five minutes' work, David takes out his book for marking by Miss Bennett: 'Yes, righto, not bad. It's a pity it's taken you such a long time to do it.' She tests him on one or two items; explains the next piece of work; ensures that he understands; exhorts him to work faster; and back he comes to his desk.

He takes an orange card with four trees on it and the word TREES and, as he settles down with this, he decides to tell me that when it was his birthday he was too frightened to go out in assembly, but he says he would not be scared now. Not for the first time today, it is evident that he is a shy, sensitive boy who finds the real world a bit much for him at times. His slowness in work cannot be attributed to laziness; he is, in fact, a hard and painstaking worker. He seems rather to have a personal speed, appropriate for him, which incorporates frequent pauses, flight into fantasy, diversions of attention. To force him to work faster seems rather like making a small car accelerate uphill while pulling a large caravan. Perhaps it can

be done, but for what purpose and at what cost? John Holt
(1967) writes:

> Timetables! We act as if children were railroad trains running on a
> schedule ... If a child doesn't arrive at one of the intermediate stations
> when we think he should, we instantly assume that he is going to be
> late at the finish. But children are not railroad trains. They don't learn
> at an even rate. They learn in spurts, and the more interested they are
> in what they are learning, the faster these spurts are likely to be.

David now has another work book and, letter by letter, copies
Wednesday from the blackboard, as he did earlier in the morning.
Seven minutes later he has completed *Wednesday 29 January*,
and is drawing four trees, meticulously colouring the trees in
different shades. At this point Miss Bennett asks three children,
including David, how many cards they have completed. David has
done one and the other two children three each. She tells him he
must have completed three by play time. He writes the words *4
trees* under his drawing and the card is complete. It has taken
seventeen minutes. Immediately he picks up the card with eight
stars on it and begins on that one.

Ever watchful, Beverley looks over my notebook. 'What you
writing?' she asks. With the amazement of an observer at a voodoo
ceremony she gasps, 'You're writing double'.

Miss Bennett now gives instructions to several children, including David, to bring her their books. She tells him he has two
seconds in which to write the word *stars* and he returns to
his desk for this purpose with no more urgency than when he
set off. He completes the star card in three minutes, apart from
the word *stars*, which he again omits, and, when it is marked,
receives instructions to do one more. All the other children are
now clearing away and lining up by the door for play time.
David selects a card with two blue kennels on it and completes
this one within three minutes, there being now only David, the
teacher and myself left in the room. His work is marked and he
is told that, as it is hardly worthwhile for him to go out and join
the others, he is to tidy the chairs during break, a task which
appears quite agreeable to him. His finished product is shown
in Figure 3.5.

At 2.50p.m. break is over and all the children, now wearing
coats and anoraks, are sitting on the floor in front of Miss Bennett,

Figure 3.5

preparing to sing some songs, including the one of John Brown's baby who had a cold upon his chest, and that of the crocodile who floated down the Nile with the lady on its back, then one of a Chinese washerwoman.

The children obviously enjoy the songs[1] and perhaps the corporate involvement which strengthens their identity as a class. Some sing and do actions; some do actions only; a few merely sit. The group singing is a very different kind of activity from most of those earlier in the day, which tended to be solitary or individual. However, the way in which 'John Brown's Baby' is sung, with varying omission of different elements, demands the same kind of concentration from the children which many of the previous activities also demanded. By contrast, the crocodile and washerwoman songs are much more relaxed and correspondingly fluent. As in assembly this morning, David looks about him, with rather a baffled air, and manages to pick up bits and pieces of appropriate song and action.

The singing lasts ten minutes and there follows a story by Miss Bennett, set in ancient Wales, about a king in a castle, surrounded by mountains and forests. The king and queen owned an enormous dog called Gelert, with huge eyes and a bell around his neck. When the king, who did not know that a dangerous wolf was nearby, had to go away for three days, the dog was left to guard the queen and the baby prince. After three days, the dog rushed out to greet his master on his return, but the king, on seeing blood around the dog's mouth, jumped to conclusions and slew Gelert with this sword. Too late he learned that the dog had, in fact, killed the wolf in a terrible fight in the baby prince's bedroom. After a few days, the king decided to erect a big pillar of stone as a monument to his faithful dog and to put on it the words:

> HERE LIES GELERT, MY GOOD AND FAITHFUL
> DOG, WHO LOOKED AFTER US ALL AND
> LOOKED AFTER MY LITTLE BABY SON.

Miss B.: And if you go to Beddgelert in Wales, you can see that stone; it's still there to this day.

The story has been well told and the children's attention well held, more by the sense of danger and savagery no doubt, than by the attribute of fidelity.

'The story' still occupies a powerful place in the primary school curriculum, and rightly so. It is a means whereby language

---

1 Teachers on the lookout for interesting classroom songs may like to dip into any of the following:

Dobbs, J., Fiske, R., Lane, M., *Ears and Eyes*, Books 1 and 2 (Oxford: OUP, 1974).
Gadsby, D., and Goldby, I., *Merrily to Bethlehem. A Very Unusual Carol Book* (London: A. & C. Black, 1978).
Green, D., *Chorus. The Puffin Colony Song Book* (Harmondsworth: Penguin: Puffin,.1977).
Harrop, B., *Apusskidu* (London: A. & C. Black, 1975).
Harrop, B., *Okki-tokki-unga. Action Songs for Children* (London: A. & C. Black, 1976).
Matterson, E., *This Little Puffin* (Harmondsworth: Penguin, 1969).

and concepts may be developed; multi-cultural and multi-ethnic awareness extended; fears assuaged; hearts touched; and the world comprehended. To do any or all of these things, the story must be appropriate. It must be capable of striking some kind of chord in the hearts and minds of the children who hear or read it and, for this to happen, the teacher must know well both stories and children. Some tales will be immediately relevant to current experience; others will speak of eternal hopes, fears, endeavours. They are interactive, educative, rich, malleable sources of enjoyment. As Barrie Wade (1986) puts it:

> Stories are a powerful force in our lives. We tell them to other people about our experiences and we listen to those that people tell us. We use stories to make sense of the world and to give us pleasure and insight. A new story can take us into other people's lives and into experiences we have never had. It can let us see how like other people we are, or how different. Stories can be talked about, retold, changed or used for our own purposes. Through them we can look back into the past or forwards into the future. Above all, they give us pleasure.

As the children button their coats ready for home, their possessions, safely guarded by the teacher, are returned to them – smokey bacon crisps; biscuits; sweets; two books, including a *Black Beauty* picture book, which Miss Bennett shows the whole group. It is now 3.15 p.m.

Miss B.:   Good afternoon, Class 4.
Children: Good afternoon, Miss Bennett. Good afternoon every-
           one.

Such politenesses are also, of course, assertions of control.

Miss B.:   Anybody whose name starts with *duh* go. Come back,
           Brian. Whose name starts with *sss* ... *a* ... *nnn* ...
           wuh ... *ruh* ... *puh* ... *kuh* ... *buh* ... *juh* ... *mmm* ...
           (*and so on*).

David, characteristically, is the last to go and, when he asks for his reading book (in the 'Janet and John' series) he remembers that he has left it at home.

At 3.30p.m. I am in the hall watching some of the children playing a game with another teacher, when a father comes to collect his child, Roy. He sees him crying and, like the king in the story, presumes the worst. In the belief that another child has hit his lad, he says 'Next time he hits you, kick him in the bloody mouth'.

Sequel 1   Theories of Learning

How may we describe and explain in more systematic, less general, terms the learning that took place while David was involved in the withdrawal remedial lesson?

Until recently it was widely assumed that children were only able to learn when they were developmentally ready for progressively more difficult tasks. This view, originating in the work of Jean Piaget (1958) has been seriously questioned and a more positive view of children's abilities is now more acceptable.

This perspective, often associated with Jerome Bruner (1973), views the child as constantly having to develop meaning from a never-ending supply of information presented by the environment. The child draws its own conclusions or makes its own hypotheses as a result of analysing the information to which it chooses to attend. The baby very quickly learns to associate information organised by its parents, especially with language and physical comfort, in the manner suggested by Robert Gagné (1977). This is by simple processes of reflexes; stimulus-response units formed by reinforcement and reward, and chains of these stimulus-response units which are formed to create more useful, larger, units of skilled behaviour.

In David's case, Gagné's more sophisticated forms of learning are seen to be operating. These forms of learning are:

(1) *Discrimination*: in relation to the information, identifying the attributes of objects, for example, so that classification is possible.

(2) *Concept learning*: This is built upon the ability to discriminate and is linked to abstraction and generalisation so as to enable manipulation of groups of similar information items, as in the work done with shapes.

(3) *Rule learning*: A rule is typically composed of several concepts, usually in a particular order. In language learning, for instance, we acquire rules for pronunciation, speaking or constructing ordered sentences.

(4) *Problem solving*: This requires the use of the other forms of learning, especially concept and rule learning, to define

103

the features of a problem and restructure what one knows to find an appropriate answer. Although it is the most complex, it occurs constantly throughout a school day and is the basis of most human activity; indeed, teaching could be defined as constant problem solving.

David brings the simple learning behaviours with him, but is required actively to attempt to give meaning to the various tasks that are presented to him and the group. The exercises in discrimination are not intended to be solved by trial and error but demand that David analyses the information in the task, considers it in relation to what he can recall from memory and then decides what is the best possible answer.

In the case of matching shapes, as in Figure 3.4, David can discriminate between the types of shape and recognises that there are two squares, but has not remembered all the information and thus does not include the triangle. This would not be unusual in many classrooms, where some children cannot assimilate all the information available and are selective about which items they recall. However, it is clear that the concepts of oblong and square are becoming familiar to David as he can identify some of their attributes.

In the case of sound discrimination, David's answer is not correct in terms of Mrs Wilder's criteria, but, considering the question, it is interesting to note that the 'wrong' answers are, in their own way, valid as answers to the 'odd one out' question. Because the answer given is not the one expected does not always reflect a lack of ability but merely a different interpretation of the information.

When David and Stacey worked together on shape matching, and with the Language Master, apart from learning the concepts and rules attached to the tasks, significant learning of a social nature is taking place. For example, some very simple understanding of co-operation and support is clearly identifiable. Moreover, the adoption of roles as questioner and answerer or commentator, as in Stacey's judgement, 'That's a good boy', seems to suggest an understanding and acceptance (to their mutual benefit) of the role of teacher and pupil.

Furthermore, probably the most important learning that is very clearly being generated in this session, is the learning about the concept of self. David's view of himself is being challenged. The way he is treated by Mrs Wilder and the rest of the group is clearly appreciative of his successes and in no way disparaging of failure. David seems to have learned that his efforts are recognised, even if they are not correct, and that help can come from peers as well as teacher; that it can be offered to others; that it can be fun. Indeed, he is valued by others and, therefore, should value himself. The importance of Mrs Wilder's expectations, whether or not explicitly stated, cannot be over-emphasised in their effect upon the children's view of themselves (Burns, 1985).

It is quite possible to develop alternative interpretations of David's learning, but this particular perspective does not lay down arbitrary levels or stages of performance. Providing there is no pathological damage, it views 'slowness' as being as much a problem of the quality of information to which the child is exposed as to a lack of ability.

Attempting to identify particular areas of difficulty in learning and providing remedial help is one of the most fascinating puzzles of teaching. However, analysing and explaining practice in terms of theory in this way is always easier in theory than in practice.

References

Burns, R. B. (1985) *Self Concept, Development and Education* (London: Holt, Rinehart and Winston).

Bruner, J. S. (1973) *Beyond the Information Given* (London: Allen & Unwin).

Gagné, R. M. (1977) *The Conditions for Learning* (London: Holt, Rinehart and Winston).

Piaget, J. (1958) *The Growth of Logical Thinking* (London: Routledge & Kegan Paul).

Sequel 2   Special Educational Needs

The following extracts are reproduced from a 1987 leaflet, by kind permission of Ian Petrie, acting on behalf of SENNAC (Special Educational Needs National Advisory Council).

Introduction

Following the recommendations of the Warnock Report (1978) and the Education Act 1981, the former statutory framework for special education based on specific categories of handicap has been replaced by the broader concept of special educational needs. The Warnock Committee estimated that approximately 20% of the school population had special educational needs, 18% being in mainstream classes (including many children whose needs had not hitherto been fully recognised) and 2% in special schools.

The definition of special educational needs in the 1981 Act is a diffuse one; children have special educational needs if they have learning difficulties which require special educational provision. The term learning difficulty refers to any kind of significant disability or limitation. The Act also encourages the integration of pupils who are currently being educated in segregated special schools.

Thus the new legislation is drawing the attention of mainstream teachers to two basic questions:

● How appropriate are current practices regarding those pupils with special educational needs who have always been in their classes?

● How capable are they of responding to the needs of pupils with more serious learning and other difficulties?

106

The Curriculum

The term curriculum is interpreted broadly to refer to the total of pupils' experience in school; in addition to the planned experiences for learning, therefore, curriculum includes informal aspects of schooling such as staff and pupil attitudes and general school ethos.

The Warnock Committee provided a useful point of departure:

> The purpose of education for all children is the same; the goals are the same. But the help that individual children need in progressing towards them will be different. Whereas for some the road they have to travel towards the goals is smooth and easy, for others it is fraught with obstacles (1.4).

The range and type of learning experiences have to be selected for their appropriateness to a child's development. The majority of children with special educational needs will require a mainstream curriculum, many needing extra support if they are to succeed with it. Some children may need considerable modifications in the presentation of their learning opportunities.

A Whole School Equal Opportunities Policy

Meeting special educational needs requires a whole school policy which stresses that all children are valued equally. Such a positive policy relates to children across the whole range of abilities, from all cultures and of both sexes.

A whole school policy seeks to provide maximal opportunities for all children. It requires personal and whole school reflection and, where needed, the eradication of attitudes which lead to low teacher expectations and the subsequent depression of motivation, aspirations and achievement in children.

STAFF INVOLVEMENT

A whole school policy of equal opportunities for maximal development involves the entire school staff, with the head teacher and senior staff working to implement the policy in all aspects of planning, practice and review. Structured and informal consultation and communication coupled with the encouragement of staff participation in the development of policy seek to achieve consensus.

In many schools a senior member of staff has already assumed responsibility for the oversight and co-ordination of the school's provision for special educational needs.

Teachers with subject responsibility in primary schools ... are responsible to the head teacher for ensuring that children with special educational needs have full access to the curriculum. This requires that syllabuses, learning materials, learning experiences and teaching strategies are sufficiently extensive and diversified to meet the range and complexity of individual needs. Those with specific responsibility for special educational needs can provide advice on the modification of text books, other learning materials and teachers' language in order to achieve a match with the functioning levels and rates of learning of children with learning difficulties. The first level of extra support has to come from the class teacher and is achieved through the deployment of an appropriate style of teaching involving a flexible repertoire.

The role of the specialist special educational needs teacher changes to a mainly advisory role in relation to the head teacher, senior management staff and class or subject staff. Some intensive direct teaching for some children may still be required, but it should be closely related to subject or project content. Special educational needs teachers may be deployed as support teachers in mainstream classes.

PARENTAL INVOLVEMENT

A whole school equal opportunities policy includes open, positive and regular contacts with parents, in order to explain what the school is doing and to exchange views on the success or otherwise of the policy in relation to their children.

INVOLVEMENT OF CHILDREN

All children are encouraged to be involved with interest and commitment in their own learning. The school's policy is crucial in creating the experience of success, recognising success and effort, adapting teaching styles to give maximal opportunities for discussion, the expression of opinions and solutions, making decisions and the involvement of children in the immediate goals of their learning.

RESPONSIBILITY OF THE SCHOOL GOVERNORS

The governors of all schools have three important duties assigned to them under the Education Act 1981. These are:

● to use their best endeavours to ensure that children with special educational needs in their school are receiving an education that caters for them properly;
● to ensure that everyone teaching children identified as having special educational needs knows about those needs and how they are to be met;
● to ensure that everyone in schools understands the importance of identifying children with special educational needs and providing for them.

LOCAL EDUCATION AUTHORITY ADVISORY AND SUPPORT SERVICES INCLUDING THE SCHOOLS PSYCHOLOGICAL SERVICE

A whole school policy seeks to achieve a balance between the school and the services which ensures that children, parents and staff have available to them any necessary or desirable expertise.

Staff Development

All courses of initial teacher training are required to contain an element on special educational needs. These courses should be strictly monitored to ensure that this element permeates all areas of the curriculum. In particular, it is essential that new entrants are aware that all school teachers are likely to be concerned with helping some children with special educational needs and that they are able to recognise the early signs of learning difficulties.

The new post-1987 in-service funding arrangements will enable a greater flexibility in the range of in-service provision and in the modes of delivery. The experience gained from the specific grant courses will facilitate an ever increasing partnership between the local education authorities and the training institutions. This will create opportunities for the further development of school-based courses and the possible establishment of regional resource centres to co-ordinate curriculum research and development.

Further Information may be obtained from: Hon. Sec. SENNAC, Hillside, 271 Woolton Road, Liverpool, L16 8NB.

Sequel 3   Teacher Training Tasks

Chapter 3 David

(1) Notice the assembly ritual for birthday children. Describe other birthday ceremonies you have met in school. What are the uses and dangers of such rituals?

(2) What kinds of teaching style does David meet in his day? What do you regard as an ideal style, and why?

(3) What, in your view, is David's most urgent need? How would you propose to try to satisfy it?

(4) Is David slow or lazy? How do you distinguish between these characteristics in children you teach or have taught? What different kinds of provision do you make for those thought to be slow, and those described as lazy?

(5) Talk about the place of 'story' in your class (or a class you know well) and list the differences between telling a story and reading a story.

(6) After scrutiny of the Sequel on 'Theories of Learning', matching it with David's experience, outline some other learning theory views which could offer different perspectives on his day.

(7) Assume that David's teachers read the Sequel on 'Special Educational Needs'. How might they subsequently modify their teaching or attitudes?

(8) In what ways should the policy and practice of your present school (or a school you know well) change in order to cater more adequately for the children with special needs?

Chapter 4

Lucy, Aged 8

*We always look at the 'Radio Times' before we
go to my nanny's, because she's got a television*

The School

Lucy's junior and infant Roman Catholic school opened with 76
children in 1967. It now has some 250 children on roll with 50
per cent from the predominantly middle-class suburban parish
and 50 per cent from outside, which makes for a good social
balance. There are seven classes, eight teachers, and a playing
field on the attractive site. Each day there is half an hour's
specialist remedial attention for the five children in each class
who are academically weakest.

The Day

It is 9.00 a.m. on a fine, fresh morning. One blast on the whistle in
the playground and the children freeze, on account of discipline
rather than climate. Another shorter bleep brings them back to
life and they line up smartly in class rows. Regular army soldiers
could hardly do better and the precision is a sign of classroom
orderliness to come.

My subject for the day is Lucy, the youngest in her class,
dressed in a turquoise blouse, grey shirt, blue tights and with a
multicoloured hair ribbon tying her fair pony tail. She moves in
line with the other 37 children (that is, 23 girls and 15 boys) to
her second-year junior classroom.

On the maths wall there are several charts. One shows 'Shapes we see every day', such as a church steeple, a stop sign, a gate, a crane. Another, again produced by the teacher, is about circles and has information by appropriate diagrams: 'All radii and diameters of the same circle are of equal length ... These are concentric circles. By how much does the diameter decrease each time?'

This is fairly demanding language for 8-year-olds. The military succinctness of the definitions, the pedagogic tone, and the uncompromising use of technical terms foreshadow the language of secondary education.

Other visual information on the same wall suggests that the definitions are not isolated and ill-digested lumps but, rather, part of a general maths context. There is also, for instance, a bar chart with coloured paper indicating squares (red); circles (fawn); rectangles (brown); triangles (yellow); ovals (green). There are ten identical copies done by the children of the same block graph. There is a variety of maths equipment, work cards and folders in a cupboard.

The reading corner includes many books donated by the Parent-Teacher Association, each with a record card which reads: ... Borrowed by; ... Returned; ... Librarian.' The choice, like the school, is catholic.

I ask one small, fair-haired, freckled boy his name and, as he tells me it is Christopher, so he screws a metal ring on his nose. This becomes a reasonably secure fixture, despite subsequent facial contortions. It is the first indication of an interesting repertoire, other parts of which Christopher will reveal as the day goes by.

The headteacher, Mr Gaskell, introduces me to the children and they seem interested and mildly excited. I believe they had been told previously to act normally, just as if I had not been there. They certainly have a brightness and a freshness, like the day, which could not have been specially assumed for the occasion, and are for the most part smartly dressed in their predominantly grey uniforms. They answer their names alertly as the attendance and dinner registers are called. There are thirty staying for dinner. Some children take the opportunity for ten minutes spelling revision before Mass. Others, maybe more confident or less wise, whisper of King Kong and Godzilla as the teacher now collects coach money for a school trip. Miss Trueman is a short, stocky, first-year probationer teacher, who has a firm, no-nonsense manner.

When the bell sounds at 9.10 a.m. she tells the girls first to line up by the door, and then the boys. Soon they are on their way down the corridor to the weekly school Mass to which parents are invited. In a denominational school of this kind, it can have the effect of strengthening the spiritual bond between children, parents and teachers. In such a setting, there is not the conflict of religious interests that might be found elsewhere, and Dearden's words (1968) may, in this context, be unexpectedly comforting. He writes: 'Prayer and worship are hollow, meaningless activities unless certain beliefs are held about the object to which they are addressed, namely God. One cannot pray or worship ABOUT religion; such activities are logically impossible apart from the presupposition of an actual belief in God.'

With the exception of the two youngest infants' classes, all the children in the school ar present as the priest, in green vestments as befits the church season, enters, flanked by two altar boys. The service, which has 'Seeing' as its theme, begins with a hymn.

> For the beauty of the earth,
> For the beauty of the skies,

Mr Gaskell conducts the singing, leads the responses and indicates when the children are to sit/stand/kneel. The priest, who is tall, elderly, and crippled, begins by telling the children that in Africa (he does not say which country), where he once worked, the people do not greet each other with 'How do you do', but instead, 'I see you'. That is to be the keynote of today's service.

The priest has an easy relationship with the children but talks rather quickly, and uses such tricky phrases, albeit with explanation, as 'beatific vision'. As he questions the whole school, so individuals respond easily and with confidence. 'How can we see Jesus? he asks. 'In the Host', replies Lucy, without hesitation. It is 'the right answer' in terms of Catholic teaching, but one wonders at the level of conceptual awareness involved in such a statement. In order to make the point more real, the priest asks a tiny boy to come out to the front and, patting him on the head, says, 'If you pull this boy's hair, you hurt Jesus. Whatever you do to him, you do to Jesus'. The idea appears to be appreciated as the bemused infant, now under advertised protection, beams his way back to his place in the ranks of the 250.

The service of mass now takes place and all except the youngest queue up to receive communion. The line includes a number of parents and teachers and the caretaker who, later in the day, will be heard moving about the school singing 'The Mountains of Mourne'.

The service, conducted with dignity and clarity, ends at 10.05 a.m. as the second and last hymn is vigorously sung, with a refrain which reinforces the day's theme of Seeing.

I know a man who's kind and gentle –

Back in the classroom, the transition from spiritual to temporal is abrupt, being effected by the teacher's words: 'We'll do maths first. That always gets us going, doesn't it?' The children greet this apparent testimony to the corporate laxative power of mathematics with 'Oooooh!' in a tone of simulated dismay, and take out their exercise books. Lucy is in a group of five.

Miss T.: Tongues away. The test was four minutes last time and four minutes the time before, so we aim for three and a half today.
Lucy: Why not three and three quarters, Miss?

In absolute silence Miss Trueman now dictates the questions and the children write the answers in their books. Here is the test which does, as Lucy requested, take three and three quarter minutes.

(1) 3 times 2   (2) 4 add 4   (3) 6 add 4
(4) 5 add 5   (5) 7 add 3   (6) 8 add 2
(7) 20 take away 10 (8) 15 take away 5 (9) 3 times 3
(10) 4 times 2   (11) 5 times 1   (12) 3 times 4
(13) 100 add 10   (14) 10 take away 7(15) 6 take away 3
(16) 8 take away 4(17) 20 take away 20(18) 10 add 3 add 6 add 1
(19) 10 times 10 (20) 19 take away 9(21) 2 times 2 add 4
(22) 18 take away 8(23) 3 times 5   (24) 3 times 4 add 12
(25) 5 times 5 add 25(26) 30 take away 10(27) 3 add 2 add 1 add 10
(28) 10 divided by 2(29) 20 divided by 2(30) 7 take away 4 add 3

The test, which begins simply, sets out to provide problems involving the four mathematical processes. Seven of the 30 items are straightforward addition, with 2 additions of 4 numbers each; 6 are multiplication; 9 subtraction; 2 division; 4 items involve a combination of processes (that is, 3 are multiplication and addition; 1 is subtraction and addition).

Confident in the knowledge of her own success, Lucy obtains the teacher's permission to distribute crayons for marking. Either in concert, or individually, children call out the answers under Miss Trueman's direction and mark their own books. In between questions there is strict silence; the whole exercise is treated very seriously indeed.

Lucy: Miss, shall we write how many we've got out of how many?

Miss T.: Yes. You know what your have to do, don't you?

There is a clearly understood sequence for this regular activity. Lucy has 30/30, as have ten to twelve other children.

Miss T.: Who has got thirty? ... twenty-nine? ... twenty-eight? ... twenty-seven? ... (*and so on*).

Christopher, who was obviously unable to concentrate during Mass, and has already twice been referred to as slow, is now praised by the teacher for his maths improvement. He has been standing by Miss Trueman's desk having his work checked and has scored 13/30. *Where* he is going wrong is not clear, since the problems combined a number of different mathematical processes. Moreover, the test itself simply reflects an attainment score. It does not diagnose weaknesses and, without the working by which his answers were arrived at, or, at least, some break-down of his wrong answers, there is no means of knowing which mathematical processes he can manage and which he cannot. Apart from that, merely asking for the scores in front of the whole class, which is done regularly throughout the land, only serves to confirm the strong in their strength and the weak in their misery, without helping either. Process, rather than answer, is more significant. Perhaps Miss Trueman checks on such process on other occasions.

With a sergeant major's abruptness, she says: 'Right, now, spelling books out' and, while the children, uninvited but aware of the system, are drawing columns in their books, she writes on the board:

er
ex
ea
ee

When all are ready, in a matter of seconds, she reads out individual words for a spelling test, arranged in groups with a common element, sometimes giving an example of the word as it might be used in a sentence. The test is as follows:

(1) *other* 'The other day I went to town.'
(2) *mother* 'Mother took me to town.'
(3) *father*
(4) *brother*
(5) *winter*
(6) *summer*
(7) *sister*
(8) *teas* (Miss T.: pronounced 'tease'.)
(9) *weave*
(10) *preach*
(11) *beneath*
(12) *cheap*
(13) *seam* 'I am going to sew the seam on my dress.'
(14) *eager* 'You are all very eager to get them right.'
(15) *leap* 'I'm going to leap with joy.' (Lucy whispers, 'Miss, that's what you said last time'.)
(16) *explain* 'Please explain to me what you are doing.'
(17) *expect* 'I expect all of you to try.'
(18) *express* 'I caught the express train.'
(19) *except* 'They all came to my party except Mary.'
(20) *excitement* 'I was full of excitement at the party.'
(21) *extinct* 'Dinosaurs are extinct.'
(22) *extra* 'You have an extra pinta today.'
(23) *extremely* 'It was extremely cold when we came here.'
(24) *extend* 'I shall extend my arm in the air.'
(25) *experiment* 'We have done an experiment.'

Numbers 1 to 7 inclusive have the *-er* sound as their common element; numbers 8 to 15 the *-ea* sound; and numbers 16 to 25 begin with the prefix *-ex*. Such careful selection of phonic items in a spelling test gives it a rationale and makes it, potentially, more of a teaching device than it would otherwise be. In this respect it contrasts with Lorraine's test in the next chapter.

After number 25 Miss Trueman says, 'OK We'll stop there', but relents in the face of the children's cry of dismay, 'Oooooh!' and, saving the best wine until last, offers two more difficult words to finish: 'Right, we'll have some more then.'

(27)   *extravagant* 'Andrew is very extravagant with his money.'
(27)   *expedition* 'Cubs and Scouts went on their expedition.'

Miss T.:   We've got to stretch your mind, haven't we, Christopher? We can't have easy ones all the time, can we, Christopher?

It is so simple for a child to be identified as the class dimwit and his inability or laziness can even become the source of innumerable jokes. One teacher I know believes that children with speech impediments should be ridiculed out of them. Some might argue that light-hearted banter in class serves the purpose of goading a pupil into producing better work. Perhaps it could, but which adult likes to be reminded of weaknesses? Perhaps all of us should, every now and again, attempt a new skill – let us say swimming, pottery, playing a musical instrument, word processing – in order to be reminded of what life is like as a learner, perhaps even as a remedial pupil.

Moreover, the surroundings in which the learning is attempted are highly significant. Success or failure may quickly become associated with a particular place, and the implications for school are obvious. 'Not only is reward satisfying and punishment annoying', writes Philip Jackson (1968) 'but, after a time, the settings in which one or the other of these conditions is continually experienced begin to engender the associated feeling on its own.'

In a highly competitive setting, the weakest come off worst. They either retreat into themselves, or develop some kind of defence mechanism. In Lucy's class, Christopher, showing varying degrees of disturbance, has chosen to be an amiable clown, rather than a nuisance. Willard Waller's comment (1932) is interesting in this respect: 'There is a tendency', he writes, 'for roles to be carried into the school room ... The clown is still a clown, but his buffoonery must be disguised; it may become covert, or it may adopt a mien of innocence and pose as blundering stupidity.'

118

The headteacher was to tell me later that Christopher, an adopted child, kicked and screamed for four weeks when he first came to school and used to hide under the table.

We now move to the marking of the spelling test. Again the children are quite familiar with the pattern. When asked, each child says the word in full and then spells it out. Christopher is first.

Miss T.:　　　Christopher, spell 'other'.
Christopher:　Other. $u - o - e - r$.

Lucy's hand shoots up like a piston, as it had done and is to do constantly throughout the day, and she whispers urgently and insistently, 'Miss, Miss'. Christopher is corrected, and so on through the list until the last three words. The excitement is now quite remarkable, verging almost on hysteria. Obviously the kudos involved in cracking one of these nuts is considerable. Suddenly it is all over, like the end of the Cup Final and, although evidence of the heightened tension lingers on, normal life may be resumed.

Lucy has 25/27, having failed at these last two hurdles, *extrava-gant* [*sic*] and *expidition* [*sic*]. She and the others on her table now discuss their errors. Christopher calls out, 'Miss, I only got seven right'. Lucy, mental arithmetic expert that she is, instantly retorts, 'You got twenty wrong then'.

It is now 10.40a.m. and, just before the bell sounds for break time, table by table the children take their spelling and maths exercise books out to the teacher. Those who remain in their seats either read their library books or do an exercise from an SRA work book. Lucy is working from page 69 of *My Own Book for Listening and Reading* (SRA Laboratory lc, *Student Record Book for Reading*, by Don H. Parker and Genevieve Scannell).

She reads each riddle very carefully, putting her finger on each word. She then consults the list and chooses the correct ones. Even though she has accounted for two of the three pictures (that is, parrot and puppy) she takes no chances with the last and again consults the list of words before deciding to write *bridge*, although that is the only picture remaining. Highly able, methodical, convergent girl that she is, she takes no risks.

There is a fifteen-minute break now for all but Miss Trueman, who is on playground duty. I write my notes in an empty classroom, drinking the coffee which the head teacher has sent with one of the girls, Elaine. With the sound of voices and screams vaguely in the distance, one has the curious feeling of being where the action isn't. A journalist two miles from the battle-front.

Not for long. At 10.55a.m. the bell sounds again and the children return, Lucy immediately taking up her SRA work book. She now tackles page 55, which is similar to page 69, except that phrases, rather than individual words, are required.

Lucy is not working sequentially through the book, page by page, but being more selective, and the children in the group recommend good pages to each other, which seems an attractive way to proceed. She now confides to the others 'There's a good one on page 78' and then works silently on her own, only looking up occasionally for the odd second. Although the children are sitting in groups, much of their work is isolated and individual.

Debbie II, opposite Lucy, is aware that the answers are printed in small lettering upside down at the bottom of the page. She sees me observe her looking at them and says to Debbie I, 'I wish they wouldn't put the answers in'. A nod in the direction of a clear conscience.

All the children, seated around double desks in groups of four or five, are now very involved, either with SRA work books or SRA work cards. The system in the class is for each child to complete a page or so and then take it to the teacher for approval, as she moves from group to group around the room. Although answers are provided for self-checking, Miss Trueman likes to keep careful track of the work herself.

One of the chief attractions of such material, as with the ubiquitous Ginn 360 is that the children are so engaged by it that the class teacher can be free to work with individuals. This is a big credit point in large or small classes and should not be underestimated. Whether the SRA scheme really develops language skills which transfer to other areas of school work and life is to be questioned. Certainly, the ability to do SRA cards will improve with practice, and perhaps the children do get a sense of progress in moving through the graded sequence of cards. However, the English language is not so linear in its development as may appear from the apparently authoritative sequence of the boxes of cards in the scheme. Moreover, work on the cards is entirely unrelated to anything else being done in school, so that a child may be doing maths work on symmetry, a project on dinosaurs, an environmental study based on the local church, but the comprehension card which, in different circumstances, could have been devised to reinforce any of these three areas, is about a bat's system of radar, or frogmen's equipment, or precious stones. Interesting topics, no doubt, but so much more meaningful if related in some way to other school activities.

On one level, SRA is merely the equivalent of a cut-up textbook, more attractively presented on durable card, in a kind of programme learning device, with amusing but non-relevant word games. On another level, it is a means whereby children may be happily occupied developing a variety of comprehension skills, while the teacher operates on a most desirable one-to-one basis. Perhaps the truth lies somewhere between these extremes.

Undeterred by such considerations, Lucy moves from SRA work book to work card. Sighing a little, she looks up at Debbie and says, 'It's only twenty past eleven'. This is the only indication all day that even stars weary sometimes. She takes the card out to Miss Trueman who asks her to read the comprehension passage entitled, 'Saved By Gum'. Lucy reads it very competently and, at the end, says, 'Ugh! I wouldn't agree with that. Chewing gum!' Dismayed by the very thought, she exchanges the card for one whose story by Rosalie Koskimaki is entitled, 'How Do Seeds Travel?' but there is no time left.

Miss T.: Let's have one table at a time, the smartest, like this one, lining up by the door.

We all move off to the school hall for a television programme and on the way two or three children talk about an old film which they enjoyed the previous Saturday on television –*King Kong and Godzilla*. Our programme today lacks the glamour of such a subject. It is on launderettes and contrasts modern washing machines with English washtubs and dollies of thirty years ago, and river washing in India.

The children watch quite attentively, sitting on the floor of a cold hall, looking at a television set whose screen reflects light in such a way that the picture is difficult to make out. All the children are in relaxed positions except Lucy, who is kneeling up and sitting back on her legs, paying particular attention, like an entranced Muslim. Miss Trueman whispers to me that Lucy does not have a television at home and is therefore all the keener to see it when she can.

After twenty minutes the rather mundane programme ends and the children return to their classroom, where Lucy immediately resumes her SRA work book.

Miss T.: Right. Everything away (*a slight snort of exasperation from Lucy*) apart from your spelling books and pencils. I said 'everything away, apart from spelling books and pencils', and that includes tongues, Caroline.

The class is to have a spelling test the following week, and they now choose ten words from the television programme just seen. Radio or television programmes need to be integrated into the curriculum and, to do this properly, requires a good deal of planning, even with video. Without such integration, they can become something akin to commercials between lessons, breathers between work sessions. In this instance, the follow-up could have taken the form of a discussion as to whose parents use the launderette, or what the children's experience of them has been; or perhaps a consideration of various washing styles and habits across time and continent; or even some critical comment on the structure and content and appeal of the television programme itself.

Miss Trueman's form of follow-up is to use the programme to provide ammunition for the next spelling session, and the following words are collected.

> *laundry*
> *launderette*
> *spin dryer*
> *weighing*
> *scales*
> *machine*
> *washed*
> *scrubbing*
> *clean*
> *fresh*

It will be a thematic spelling test this time, rather than a phonic item test, as before.

Miss T.: Any more?

Debbie: Soap.
Miss T.: How do you spell it, Debbie?
Debbie: $s - o - u - p$.

The children quickly realize that this is not what most people wash with and there is general amusement.

As they call out their suggestions, so the teacher accepts some, such as those just mentioned, and rejects others, including:

> *filthy*
> *television*
> *fifteen minutes*

The criteria for acceptance or rejection is not clear.

There are two minutes left before the bell at 12.00p.m. to signify the end of a morning school spent largely on what some might call 'basic skills'. It is an unhelpful and ill-considered cliché, implying in theory some clearly defined and universally accepted foundations on which all else is built. In practice, meaning spelling, punctuation, sentence structure and simple computational competence. None of which is to be derided but, equally, not raised above its station either. 'Basic' equipment for mountaineers means that without which they cannot possibly climb mountains. What is 'basic' equipment for a school pupil? It is certainly not easily determined, but it might include a measure of oral ability; a reasonable store of appropriate words; an ability to comprehend appropriate reading matter; to communicate one's thoughts, ideas and wishes adequately in writing; a general grasp of what numbers do and how they may be manipulated; a degree of socialization. Technique and technical competence (terms which are preferable to 'basic skills') come later.

Finally, this morning, in response to the teacher's invitation for a song title, Michele suggests, 'I Went to the Animal Fair', and this is what they sing.

The song becomes a round, and half the class repeats 'monkey', while the other half sings the verse again. When tried a third time, it becomes a bit chaotic, but is obviously enjoyed by the children, who are furiously performing the actions as well as singing.

Miss T.: Erm. Sometimes you sing as though a funeral march was going by, without any gaiety about you so far.

There is a remarkably powerful corporate identity about the class. The children act as one well-disciplined and organized unit, responding to the teacher's commands, rebukes and jokes. The highly competitive spirit appears to please many of the boys and girls. One wonders what its long-term effects will be, on all the children, but particularly the weaker ones such Christopher.

The bell sounds and the children stand up behind their chairs, some preparing for school dinner, others, like Lucy, to go home.

Miss T.: If our country depended on you we'd be in a poor way, you don't stand up straight.
Child: Miss, you don't stand up at war.

Miss Trueman acknowledges such logic with good grace.

With that, we move again to the school hall which had previously doubled as a church, and television room, and now serves as a dining space. Outside in the foyer stand four boys, spaced apart from each other like redundant chess pieces, awaiting or enduring punishment. Miscreants on show. Inside all is activity.

The head teacher and I sit with four children, and behind us are the remains of a jumble sale which one class has organized. A grand total of £10.27p has been raised for a village in Peru devastated by earthquake. By such altruistic work is children's natural generosity harnessed; their moral awareness extended; their concern for others, near and far, developed. Every school has a few honourable tales to tell of charitable work done by teachers as well as pupils.

Dinner is supervised by non-teaching helpers who come into school for an hour or so per day. Today we have potatoes, dumplings, stew, and semolina with currants.

After the meal there is the Grace. Then, for the children, activities in the playground; for me, note-making in the classroom. While I am so engaged, Lucy and friend walk by the window and give a wave. It is a further sign, if one were needed, of confidence on her part since, up to this point, we have only exchanged a few words.

At 1.27p.m. the playground whistle sounds and an ancillary's desperate scream, 'Will you be quiet', is heard twice. At 1.30p.m. the school bell rings and the third person to enter the classroom is Lucy, looking fresh and healthy. Another child shows me her jumble sale spoils: a little vase for 3p; a record for 10p; a photocard for 1p. Treasures indeed.

Miss Trueman now gives instructions for the half-hour period proceeding PE. She will see some children individually for maths and the rest may choose between an SRA work book or work card and their reading book. Lucy elects to continue with her SRA card *How Do Seeds Travel?* A boy comes to borrow a crayon.

Boy: Can I have blue, Lucy?
Lucy: Yeah. Bring it back.

Debbie II overhears the teacher ask two pupils to ask Class 7 to prepare the apparatus for PE and says, 'Great, we haven't had that for ages'.

Miss Trueman now (that is, 1.39p.m.) calls the register, boys' names first, and the children appear easily able to carry on with their work and answer, 'Yes, Miss', at the time their name is called, without any attention being diverted from their tasks. They all work in a very concentrated manner, whispering occasionally.

Lucy now returns the SRA 9 Lime Lab. 1c card to the box on the nature table and, having checked her answers, chooses another card, Lime 11, with a story by Ellen Cafferata entitled, *A Mystery Tower*. She begins work on this immediately and when Andrew, thinking out loud, asks, 'What's the date today?' she instantly replies, without breaking her concentration, 'The twenty-fourth'. She reads through the twenty-two-line story and then tells Andrew, 'I've only got two more to do and then I've finished Lime'. She completes the card apart from the final section, which requires a piece of imaginative writing. When I ask her the reason for this omission, she tells me 'Because Miss says it takes too long'.

This is unfortunate, unless there are other opportunities for the kind of writing that allows children free rein to explore their imaginative and fantasy worlds, as well as their feelings and attitudes, or indeed, for continuous prose writing of any kind. Over the last twenty years, written work of an incredibly high quality, emanating from children across the ability ranges in primary schools up and down the land, has been published in a variety of anthologies. Much has been learnt about how to tap this rich vein of experience and skill.

Miss Trueman, seated at her desk, continues to interview individual children, hearing them read; checking their maths books; helping in other matters, until 2.02p.m.

Miss T.: Right. Put everything away, including tongues, Richard. The quieter we are, the faster we shall go.

Her assertion may now be tested as the children go off to bring PE clothes back to the classroom. She advises me that, as some of the girls are rather shy, she always 'vacates' at this point. I take the hint and disappear for a minute or so while the boys and girls change, speculating on the self-awareness of 8-year-olds.

At 2.10p.m. all the children enter the hall very quietly and sit in separate spaces on the floor. The PE apparatus has been set out by older boys from Class 7 in readiness: a buck (or horse) and mats; a climbing frame; a sloping ladder with mats; a device resembling a decorator's ladder with planks. The hall is now a gymnasium substitute. It seems wise to make such varied use of such a large space. Necessity becomes a virtue.

The boys and girls are all dressed in shorts and singlets, some of an idiosyncratic kind. Christopher's, with a monkey on the front, proclaims 'Pass the monkey wrench'. Under the teacher's direction the children begin by jumping on the spot sixty times to warm up. It certainly is very cold. They then step on the spot, knees up high, before moving to the gym apparatus, a prospect which excites them all. It is the equivalent of cake after bread and butter.

Lucy, in a group of ten, first tries the sloping bench. She jumps up on the bench, two feet at a time, and then, sitting down, slides from top to bottom. This is different from what everyone else does. Next she moves to the buck and mat, where the activity is more uniform. She jumps up on the buck ... stops ... leaps into the air ... and, after landing on her feet, does a forward roll on the mat. When all the children have tried this, they change to jumping over the buck. Lucy catches her foot initially and is momentarily disconcerted. She moves to the climbing frame, going up high near the ceiling and, a little later, to the decorator's ladder.

She is, in fact, well co-ordinated, being tall for her age and quite athletic. The best group academically (including Lucy) is also more assured and proficient at these physical activities. However, to think in terms of groups, instead of individuals, is as dangerous in PE as in other areas of the curriculum and some words of caution from the Department of Education and Science are appropriate.

A wide variation in height, weight, ability and interest is to be found in children of the same age, and different stages of development are represented in a random selection of children of similar age and physique. Achievement depends on the stage of development a child has reached as well as on his innate ability, and it is difficult to forecast the pattern and extent of his future progress. Teaching in physical education, as in other aspects of the curriculum, must therefore be closely related to individual needs and differences, but it is also of value to teachers to know and recognise those characteristics that the majority of children have in common. (1972)

By contrast with Lucy and her group, Christopher is performing very badly, but enjoying himself enormously and trying hard. Different children have differing levels and kinds of satisfaction. At 2.35p.m. he is sent back to the classroom early for some offence, like a soccer player given his marching orders. He goes without a murmur, but is clearly disappointed.

Ten minutes from time there is a short interlude when individual children demonstrate their skills in front of their peers. Then, after a few more minutes of corporate involvement, it is 2.45p.m. and playtime. The children return to their classroom to change, with some of the boys debating whether to play soccer or hot rice in the playground. Ever vigilant, Lucy reminds me that I had planned to have a chat with her and, for the first few minutes of break, we talk about her home and interests and school. What Lucy says, if not its style, reminds me of something I had forgotten – that, despite her poise and confidence, she is still an 8-year-old. Here is part of the conversation.

R. M.: Tell me, Lucy, tell me about your family.
Lucy: Well, my daddy's a solicitor. And my mum she doesn't go out you see. I've got two brothers. Henry and John and Henry is ten, eleven in June, and John's nine, he's ten in June.
R. M.: How do the brothers treat you? Do they treat you well?
Lucy: O.K. I'm glad that I'm having a friend tonight then because John has to sleep in my room for a bit because his room's being decorated.

127

R. M.: Yes, and you've got a friend staying with you?

Lucy: Yes. She's got to sleep in John's bed. Her name's Stephanie.

R. M.: I see. Mmm. Now tell me, what sort of things are you interested in, Lucy?

Lucy: Swimming and I like to draw and I play with dominoes. I made a zoo out of dominoes yesterday and put zoo animals in them.

R. M.: That sounds very good. I've played dominoes, but I've never made a zoo out of dominoes.

Lucy: And we build dominoes into a set and then knock down end, knock down one piece of dominoes and it all fall down and we tried to use up all the dominoes but what happened was when we were putting the last piece, no not the last, there were about five less, left and it fell down.

R. M.: Fell down before you'd finished it?

Lucy: Yes.

R. M.: What about, erm, what about today? You think of the sort of day you've had at school today. Is it a normal kind of day?

Lucy: Yes. Yes.

R. M.: Quite normal?

Lucy: Yes.

R. M.: What sort of things did you like best in it, that have happened so far?

Lucy: The television programme and PE and I liked it when we were doing SRA. When we were doing the activity page at the back.

R. M.: Yes. Why do you like those?

Lucy: Because the code and things like that, they're interesting.

R. M.: You like that, mmm. Why do you like the television?

Lucy: Because it's interesting and it tells you about things.

R. M.: Mmm. Mmm. And I think Miss Trueman said you hadn't got a television at home.

Lucy: No.

R. M.: Is that right? Do you miss it?

Lucy: Not really, because I'm not used to it, except we always look at the *Radio Times* before we go to my nanny's because (*R. M. laughs*) she's got a television.

R. M.: So you watch it at your nanny's, do you?

Lucy: Yes. And at our friends' houses.

R. M.:   ... And you liked the PE? I thought you did well at PE. You seemed to enjoy that didn't you? Which things did you like best in it?

Lucy: The climbing frame.

R. M.:   Yes. I thought you'd probably like that because you went up quite high, didn't you?

Lucy: Went over the top.

R. M.:   Over the top. Right near the ceiling.

Lucy: The infants have a ribbon tied on to one of the bars and they're not to go higher than the ribbon.

R. M.:   I see. On that same frame?

Lucy: Yes.

R. M.:   Well, that's quite a good idea, isn't it?

This is far from a normal conversation. It is more of a gentle interrogation, with Lucy providing the answers. But there is plenty of evidence here of her ability to extend a point and develop a suggestion, drawing on her own experience; of her easy rapport with a relative stranger; of her preparedness to take the initiative in the exchange; of the fact that she knows her own mind and can answer both closed and open questions with precision and clarity and speed.

Lucy is as alert and keen now as at the beginning of the day. Since 9.00a.m. she has constantly been picking up the smallest detail and, despite being occupied in a variety of tasks, has heard virtually every word her teacher has spoken. This is no special performance for my benefit for the way in which it has been sustained is perfectly natural for her lively personality and sharp mind and, as she said to me in our conversation just now, 'Miss told us to think of it as a normal day as if you weren't there, because just to show how we normally are'. And Lucy is a girl who does as she is told.[1]

---

1   She is also what some would term a 'gifted' child and anyone interested in this concept might refer to the National Association for Curriculum Enrichment and Extension, c/o J. B. Teare, Newell Grange High School, Greenbrow Road, Wythenshawe, Manchester M23 8SX, and to:

Freeman, J. (1986) *The Psychology of Gifted Children* (New York: Wiley).
Leydon, S. (1986) *Helping the Child of Exceptional Ability* (London: Croom Helm).
Ogilvie, E. (1975) *Gifted Children in Primary Schools* (London: Macmillan).

She goes outside for the last few minutes of break time before 3.00p.m. when the whole class returns for an activity which is familiar to them, an exercise devised by SRA and intended to develop listening skills. The system is that the children concentrate their attention solely on a picture in front of them while the teacher reads out, in a good clear voice, a story relevant to that picture. Questions follow on the factual content of the story and the children underline their answers from a multiple choice set of alternatives. It is, thus, a piece of artificially contrived concentration, which makes use of material of the kind normally written to be read silently, rather than aloud.

The fact that Lucy's answers, including the sequence of events of the narrative, are all correct, leads one to wonder yet again if her mind is being challenged. Few, if any, of her tasks throughout this day have been open-ended.

Ten other children also give totally correct responses which, in this instance, is 8/8 since, as Lucy was the first to point out to Miss Trueman, responses three and four involve a misprint and are, therefore, omitted by all children. Instead of blotting such a misprint out of their consciousness, the children could have written to the SRA publishers about it. It would have been a chance to write to a real reader for a real purpose.

Some boys and girls do not do so well with the test. Our friend Christopher sits at his desk throughout the whole sequence of events, with his head on his arms; no picture in front of him; answering no questions. Is he sulking after the PE rebuke, or tired, or merely feeling unco-operative for no particular reason? Contrast him with Lucy, sitting bolt upright on her chair, hands clasped in her lap, looking fixedly at the picture as if it were a crystal ball with the key to all mysteries. Chance members of the same school class, they are worlds apart in outlook and personality, required to act with the rest of the class in unison.

Certainly, such activities where thirty boys and girls act as one have a value. They emphasize the corporate unity of the class and establish its identity with security. They signify to the teacher the ground which she has attempted to cover with all the pupils in her care. But they have their problems, too. Not least, that an activity which interests or stretches one child may bore or bewilder another, as happens here. Hence the argument for a diversity of tasks at times and for more individualised treatment. Particularly, perhaps, in this context. 'We cannot support the kind of "listening exercise"', says Bullock 'which is applied to a whole

130

class, irrespective of individual capacity and need ... Wherever we saw this being practised ... the able children could have been given more demanding listening experience, and the slow learners suffered from having their inadequacies made public' (para. 10.21, 1975).

Miss Trueman's preference, however, is for the common assignment, so that she and the children know where they stand. She is a strict disciplinarian with a sharp tongue, a firm manner and a sense of humour. The children like her, respond with alacrity, and obey her instructions.

The *Listening Skill Builder* exercise lasts half an hour and, when the marking is complete, the children take out their music books for singing at the end of the day. The song chosen is ideal for a class activity involving, as it does, a cast of several (if not thousands), mime and drama, and a clear narrative.

Christopher gives me his watch to look after. Does he feel things could get too boisterous for his Timex, as he plays the lead role of Mr Frog goin' a courtin'? Other parts are distributed by the teacher with a firmness (and corresponding compliance) which film producers would envy, and very excited children take up their positions, having pushed back the desks to allow space for movement. The chorus sings the words and the principals, with Lucy as uncle Rat, mime their parts in a well-understood sequence, culminating in a holocaust reminiscent of Hamlet.

> A frog went a-courting, he did ride,
> Hum-hum. Hum-hum.

Miss T: Well, considering that we haven't done it since November, that was quite good. Quite good. I still think Mr Jennings (*i.e. Christopher*) thinks that the whole show should be his.

By popular request they repeat the song, with different children taking the character parts.

Miss T.: This time I expect more singing from the class. Everyone sit down then.
Frog – Geoffrey;
Uncle Rat – Richard;
Big black bug – Jane;

Rattlesnake – Martin;
Bumble bee – Sarah;
Hoppity flea – Alison;
Old tom cat – Louise;
Big black snake – Donald.
Now, if you're not going to do this properly and with more spirit than last time, I think I'll have to stop you. Right. All of us sing. Even the wedding guests. O.K. One, two, three.

Children: A frog went a-courting, he did ride,
Hum-hum. Hum-hum.
(And so on.)

Smiles and grins testify that the first-night performance was just as enjoyable as the dress rehearsal. Lucy sings quite strongly, if off-key occasionally, and is an obvious leader in the singing.

Finally, an appropriate song at the end of the day about sleeping and waking:

4.00p.m. The bell sounds and the children stand and face the classroom crucifix.

Children: Hail, Mary, full of grace,
The Lord is with thee;
Blessed art thou among women,
And blessed is the fruit of thy womb, Jesus.
Holy Mary, Mother of God,
Pray for us sinners
Now and at the hour of our death.
Amen.

The grace of our Lord Jesus Christ,
And the love of God,
And the fellowship of the Holy Ghost,
Be with us all, now and for ever. Amen.

Miss T.: Goodnight, children.
Children: Goodnight, Miss Trueman. Goodnight, Mr Mills.
R. M.: Goodnight children. Thank you for having me.
Christopher: I thought you'd say that.

Sequel 1   Suggested Fiction

Collections

Benjamin, Floella (1984) *Why the Agouti Has no Tail and Other Stories* (London: Hutchinson).
Bond, Ruskin (1982) *Tales and Legends from India* (London: Julia MacRae).
Crouch, Marcus (1983) *The Whole World Storybook* (Oxford: OUP).
Elkin, Judith (1983) *The New Golden Land Anthology* (London: Viking Kestrel).
Hamilton, Virginia (1986) *The People Could Fly* (London: Walker).
Jaffrey, Madhur (1985) *Seasons of Splendour* (London: Pavilion).
Lewis, Naomi (1986) *The Flying Trunk and Other Stories from Andersen* (London: Andersen Press).
Singh, Rani (1984) *The Indian Storybook* (London: Heinemann).
Starkey, Dinah (1985) *Ghosts and Bogles* (London: Heinemann).
Williams-Ellis, Amabel (1983) *The Story Spirits* (London: Pan).

Five to Seven-Year-Olds

Agard, John (1981) *Dig Away Two-Hole Tim* (London: Bodley Head).
Ahlberg, Janet and Ahlberg, Allan (1978) *Each Peach Pear Plum* (London: Viking Kestrel).
Bang, Molly (1983) *Ten Nine Eight* (London: Julia MacRae).
Blake, Quentin (1980) *Mister Magnolia* (London: Cape).
Bradman, Tony (1986) *Through My Window* (London: Methuen).
Briggs, Raymond (1978) *The Snowman* (London: Hamish Hamilton).
Brown, Ruth (1981) *A Dark, Dark Tale* (London: Andersen Press).
Burningham, John (1984) *Granpa* (London: Cape).
Burningham, John (1978) *Would You Rather* (London: Cape).
Cole, Babette (1986) *Princess Smartypants* (London: Hamish Hamilton).
Cole, Babette (1983) *The Trouble with Mum* (Kingswood: Kaye and Ward).
Counsel, June (1984) *But Martin!* (London: Faber).
Daly, Niki (1985) *Not so Fast, Sungololo* (London: Gollancz).

Dodd, Lynley (1983) *Hairy Maclary From Donaldson's Dairy* (Barnstaple: Spindlewood).

Flournoy, Valerie (1985) *The Patchwork Quilt* (London: Bodley Head).

Fox, Mem (1986) *Wilfred Gordon Mcdonald Partridge* (London: Viking Kestrel).

Ganly, Helen (1986) *Jyoti's Journey* (London: André Deutsch).

Gray, Nigel (1985) *I'll Take You to Mrs Cole* (London: Andersen Press).

Hersom, Kathleen (1983) *Maybe It's a Tiger* (London: Macmillan).

Hill, Eric (1980) *Where's Spot* (London: Heinemann; dual language editions: Baker Books).

Hoban, Russell (1977) *Dinner at Alberta's* (London: Cape).

Hughes, Shirley (1977) *Dogger* (London: Bodley Head).

Hughes, Shirley (1979) *Up and Up* (London: Bodley Head).

Jones, Terry (1981) *Fairy Tales* (London: Pavilion).

Le Cain, Erroll (1984) *Hiawatha's Childhood* (London: Faber).

McKee, David (1980) *Not Now Bernard* (London: Andersen Press, dual language editions: Baker Books).

Murphy, Jill (1980) *Peace at Last* (London: Macmillan).

Oram, Hiawyn (1982) *Angry Arthur* (London: Andersen Press).

Ormerod, Jan (1981) *Sunshine* (London: Viking Kestrel).

Pressman, Lee (1985) *Muckfield's Midnight Monster Match* (London: Dent).

Ross, Tony (1986) *I Want My Potty* (London: Andersen Press).

Varley, Susan (1984) *Badger's Parting Gifts* (London: Andersen Press).

Vesey, A. (1985) *The Princess and The Frog* (London: Methuen).

Wallace, Ian (1984) *Chin Chiang and The Dragon's Dance* (London: Methuen).

Walsh, Jill Paton (1982) *Babylon* (London: Dent).

Willis, Jeanne (1986) *The Monster Bed* (London: Andersen Press).

Yeoman, John and Blake, Quintin (1979) *The Wild Washerwoman* (London: Hamish Hamilton).

Eight to Eleven-Year-Olds

Ahlberg, Allen (1985) *Ten In a Bed* (London: Granada). Series of stories based around nursery rhyme characters.

Ahlberg, Janet and Ahlberg, Allan (1986) *The Jolly Postman* (London: Heinemann). Innovative design with plenty of humour in the distinctive Ahlberg style.

Ashley, Bernard (1981) *Dinner Ladies Don't Count* (London: Julia MacRae). A realistic school setting and just enough text for the young reader to enjoy.

Banks, Lynne Reid (1980) *The Indian in the Cupboard* (London: Dent). A magic cupboard brings alive a miniature Red Indian.

Browne, Anthony (1983) *Gorilla* (London: Julia MacRae). Picture book for the older reader with a host of eccentric detail in the illustrations.

Cameron, Ann (1982) *The Julian Stories* (London: Gollancz). Two black brothers and their father provide the situations in this warmly defined book.

Cherrington, Clare (1984) *Sunshine Island Moonshine baby* (London: Collins). A collection of events from the West Indies told to a young girl.

Cross, Gillian (1981) *Save Our School* (London: Methuen). Three friends fight to save their school from closure.

Crossley-Holland, Kevin (1986) *Storm* (London: Heinemann). Prize winning ghost story with a short but absorbing narrative.

Doherty, Berlie (1982) *How Green You Are!* (London: Methuen). Humour is attractively provided within a realistic inner city setting.

Gardam, Jane (1981) *Bridget and William* (London: Julia MacRae). Deceptively simple story about a girl and a horse, set in the North.

Godden, Rumer (1983) *The Valiant Chatti Maker* (London: Macmillan). The renowned story-teller with a book set in her beloved India.

Hughes, Shirley (1985) *Chips and Jessie* (London: Bodley Head). The much lauded illustrator has here provided a humorous story about two friends, with plenty of comic strip techniques.

Kaye, Geraldine (1984) *Comfort Herself* (London: Dent). The story of a young girl who is half-English and half-Ghanian and what happens to her after her mother's death.

Kemp, Gene (1977) *The Turbulent Term of Tyke Tiler* (London: Faber). Modern school story with a surprise twist in its ending.

King-Smith, Dick (1983) *The Sheep-Pig* (London: Gollancz). Warm and funny farmyard tale about a pig who thinks it is a sheepdog.

McGough, Roger (1982) *The Great Smile Robbery* (London: Viking Kestrel). Hilarious and slapstick book by one of the great stylists of children's writing.

Mahy, Margaret (1981) *Raging Robots and Unruly Uncles* (London: Dent). Typically quirky story by the New Zealand writer about two families and their inventions.

Mark, Jan (1980) *Nothing to be Afraid Of* (London: Viking Kestrel). Set of slightly creepy stories, told with much wicked wit.

Munsch, Robert (1982) *The Paper Bag Princess* (London: Hippo). A resourceful princess heroine is involved in a series of amazing events.

Naidoo, Beverley (1985) *Journey to Jo'burg* (London: Longman). A painfully realistic book about the cruelties of apartheid.

Nimmo, Jenny (1986) *The Snow Spider* (Longman: Methuen). Short but absorbing story about a boy's search for his dead sister.

Pearce, Philippa (1978) *The Battle of Bubble and Squeak* (London: André Deutsch). Domestic drama about family conflicts surrounding two gerbils.

Thompson, Brian (1980) *The Story of Prince Rama* (London: Viking Kestrel). Superb illustrations in traditional Indian style accompany this story from a religious classic.

Waddell, Martin (1983) *Going West* *(London: Andersen Press)*. Told in comic strip form, this is the story of settlers in the American West.

Walsh, Jill Paton (1985) *Gaffer Samson's Luck* (London: Viking Kestrel). Beautifully constructed story about the friendship between a boy and an old man.

Information About Books

Bookquest. Three issues per annum. The Literacy Centre, Brighton Polytechnic, Falmer, Sussex.

Books for keeps. Six issues per year. School Bookshop Association, 1 Effingham Road, Lee, London SE12 8NZ.

British Book News Children's Books. Quarterly. British Council, 65 Davies Street, London W1Y 2AA.

Material Matters. Nine issues per annum. Hertfordshire Library Service, County Headquarters, Hertfort SG13 8EJ.

Tried and tested. Three issues per annum. CLPE, Ebury Teacher's Centre, Sutherland Street, London SW1 4LII.

Sequel 2   Ten Strategies for Story

Have a Rich Variety of Books

Tolerance, identification and understanding of a rich diversity of stories are important positive outcomes of using stories set in other cultures.

All children enjoy:

- folk tales, myths, and legends from many lands;
- stories set in other times and cultures;
- listening to stories in their first language;
- listening to taped stories in English;
- retelling legends and traditional stories.

Try the following

- taping stories in English so children can read and listen;
- encouraging parents to tell stories in both first language and English;
- encouraging older brothers and sisters to do the same;
- making dual-text story books.

(1)   obtain written translations from someone in the community.
(2)   insert these on cards or (more successfully) on strips stuck under or above the English text.
(3)   obtain taped readings of the story translations.

Read Yourself!

Enjoy your own stories; let children see your satisfaction and share it with them. Keep a book you are enjoying on your desk and let children see you reading it occasionally. Children are not fools and it's surprising how often what we recommend fails to take root because we don't do it ourselves.

Some schools have successfully experimented with USSR (not a subversive activity, but Uninterrupted Sustained Silent Reading). At a specific time in the week everyone in the whole school stops what they are doing and picks up a book for about twenty quiet minutes. 'Everyone' means just that, including head teacher, secretary, caretaker and any parents or advisers who may be there at the time!

● enthuse about books and the pleasure they give you;
● talk about books you have read;
● be honest about those you didn't enjoy.

Make Time for Reading

Sharing books together is a focal point of whole class activities.

● Read aloud frequently and, if enough texts are not available, occasionally put short passages on an overhead projector for all to follow;
● Give time throughout the week for browsing through the class library and maybe use the books there to develop individualized reading;
● Don't be afraid to let children take books home from the very beginning of reading. That's where most sustained reading will be done.

Encourage Pleasure not Pressure

Very young school children can distinguish between 'real' books and 'reading' books. Some reading schemes used in classrooms say to children 'reading is boring' because their books are boring. Check your schemes are based upon

● the language people use in real life;
● forward moving, coherent narratives;
● stories that give pleasure in themselves.

If they are not, seek to change them.

No amount of pressure to complete (or compete to finish) a scheme can make up for a lack of pleasure in reading. We are in the business of creating readers for a lifetime, not forcing children to jump through the hoops of a graded scheme for their own sake. So

- start with the expectation that reading is fun;
- give children chance to talk about their pleasure;
- let a child change a book that has become boring or stale.

Polish Your Own Skills

Celebrate story by recreating moods and feelings as well as the ideas behind words on the printed page. Work on your skills as a story teller and story reader.

STORY TELLING

- pick a story you really enjoy;
- try it out a few times (in front of a mirror can help);
- use all your resources (movement, voice, gesture, facial expression);
- involve the children (joining in repetitions and choruses, guessing what will happen);
- use aids, puppets or illustrations (try simple sketches on the blackboard or overhead projector as you go);

STORY READING

An expressive, fluent reading by the teacher is the best way to help children recreate a story's meaning. Some hints:

- know the story well (so that you can dramatize it effectively);
- try out a reading to get the feelings right;
- experiment with different voices for different characters;
- check all children are sitting so that they can see you (your expressions and eye-contact can be important) and, if necessary, the illustrations (a compact group is better than isolated children in rows);
- Don't interrupt your story by asking questions. When you have finished, these will come from the children.

Try These Follow-Up Activities

Sometimes it's best to have no systematic follow-up. After all, enjoyment of literature is the main aim and we don't want to overkill. Remember the boy who saw the rabbit on a nature walk. 'Quick', said his friend, 'look the other way or Miss'll make us write about it.'

Children can

- tell each other about similar experiences in their own lives;
- write a sequel;
- talk in small groups (without an adult) about the story and the people in it;
- design a paperback cover;
- retell the story perhaps from one character's view;
- make a radio drama of a scene;
- act out a scene;
- write about their feelings as they read or listen;
- illustrate the story in pictures round the walls;
- make puppet characters and use them to enact the story.

Encourage Storytelling by Children

Oral stories are an important part of our culture and literature. Encourage a relaxed atmosphere for:

- exchange of anecdotes, jokes, yarns, experiences;
- retelling of well-known stories;
- invention of new stories;
- children in groups take it in turns to tell part of a story.

Make sure you listen attentively and the children know you do.

Use Rhymes and Rhythm

Use plenty of nursery and playground rhymes. They are fun. They work through repetition and the patterns of rhythm and sound. Also they are frequently stories in themselves.

- use them on overhead projectors as alternatives to reading primers;
- speak them aloud;
- do the actions;
- mime the expressions and feelings;
- make up more rhymes and verses together;
- read lots of poetry aloud;
- work together on class poems.

Make Children into Writers

Let children write their own stories from the early years. They have plenty of experience of what a story is from their own games, anecdotes and stories they have heard. So

- have a special book for stories or have loose leaves pinned together in an illustrated cover;
- tape record or write down yourself the spoken stories of children who have severe difficulty with the mechanics of writing;
- encourage children to revise their drafts;
- sometimes allow children to revise each other's drafts;
- encourage small groups to work on writing collaboratively;
- make up stories as a whole class.

Help Children to Internalize and Recreate Stories

Encourage your pupils to try the following:

- close your eyes, picture, then draw a story character (then talk about differences);
- on one piece of paper show all the connections between people and events (then talk about relationships in the story);
- make a wall-poster of illustration and text (rewritten by children, then typed) of a story, so that it can be read;
- after one reading or telling children draw *then cut out* different characters and things in a story; (then, as you retell the story, use the blackboard as a scene, allowing

141

children to stick on their own cut-out with Blu-tack at the appropriate time and in the appropriate position);
- recreate a story through improvization (or make puppet characters for acting it out);
- make a story streamer – a long sheet folded for each event depicted. (The Bayeux tapestry is an example without folds!) Draw the scenes without worrying about producing works of art. (Then talk about sequence or use the streamers as prompts for children's own retelling.)
- storyswitch in pairs with teacher directing. Use a well-known story which one child in each pair begins to tell. When teacher signals (e.g. hand clap) the other takes over exactly where the first finished and so on. (Don't try this if you can't stand laughter.) (Adapted from Barrie Wade's book *Story at Home and School*, Educational Review publication, University of Birmingham, 1984.)

Sequel 3 Teacher Training Tasks

Chapter 4 Lucy

(1) Having first read the 'School Assembly' Sequel, discuss the way in which Lucy's school assembly is different.

(2) What evidence is there that Lucy is intelligent? How do you distinguish between intelligence and conformity to teacher's demands?

(3) The need to provide stimulating work for the more able child has been highlighted in several reports of Her Majesty's Inspectorate. Is Lucy intellectually challenged during the day, or merely going through the motions, or perhaps consolidating her knowledge?

(4) How do you account for the atmosphere in her class? What are its chief characteristics? What kind of atmosphere do you try to promote in your class?

(5) What do you understand by the term 'basic skills'. To what extent is it a helpful and a misleading concept?

(6) What are the traditional and more modern aspects of Lucy's day?

(7) Consider the amount of time Lucy spends on different areas of the curriculum. Assuming the pattern is repeated in the rest of the week, does the proportion seem to be in line with the national curriculum?

(8) Drawing on your own experience of stories which have been well received by children, add half a dozen titles to the list of 'Suggested Fiction' in the Sequel.

(9) Scrutinise the Sequel 'Ten Strategies for Story', in terms of your own views, by listing points made in a two-column checklist of (a) Ideas Tried/Attitudes Shared, and (b) New Ideas/Different Attitudes. Then try out a couple of the new ideas.

(10) Lucy is not encouraged to do the piece of imaginative writing on the SRA card. What are your views on this?

What part can personal writing play in the curriculum, in terms of:

(a) doing things for real purposes;
(b) becoming aware of the needs of an audience;
(c) gaining practice in a range of forms and genres;
(d) drafting and re-drafting, as professional writers do;
(e) developing a personal voice;
(f) gaining benefits from process as well as product.

(11) A survey into teachers' aims by Pat Ashton, *et al.* (1975) produced the following list, in order of priority:

(a) Children should be happy, cheerful and well balanced.
(b) They should enjoy school work and find satisfaction in their achievements.
(c) Individuals should be encouraged to develop in their own ways.
(d) Moral values should be taught as a basis of behaviour.
(e) Children should be taught to respect property.
(f) They should be taught courtesy and good manners.
(g) They should be taught to read fluently and accurately.
(h) They should be read appropriate material with understanding.

Commenting on these aims, Dearden (1976) writes: 'No reference to maths, science, the arts, PE, or languages in the eight most important aims. With the exception of reading and moral education, there is a total concentration on attitudes, to the exclusion of content.'

How do these aims seem to match the experiences recorded in Lucy's day, or in any of the other days in this book?

Explain, with your reasons, how you would rank these eight aims.

What do you feel about Dearden's comment?

Chapter 5

Lorraine, Aged 9

We had a bird, but it died on Friday

The School

There are 474 other junior children in Lorraine's school, along with a head teacher; fourteen full-time staff; one part-time special needs teacher; and no less than four part-time needlework teachers. A rather curious phenomenon, which means that craft activities must be sex-orientated. A separate infants school of some 200 children is on the same site and serves the entirely suburban, owner-occupier, catchment area. The junior school, which has been academically very successful for many years, is unstreamed by design. In other words, all children are tested after their first year and then grouped according to age, sex and ability, to produce a balance within each class. In addition, certain children are extracted in small groups each day for a quarter of an hour's extra reading, and each is heard individually. All buildings and grounds are modern, attractive and well cared for.

The Day

It is a bright, sunny yet cold-ish Friday at the end of November, and the focus of attention for today is Lorraine, who is quite smartly dressed in the blue and grey school uniform, blue and yellow tie, white shirt, blue cardigan, white knee-length socks and brown shoes. She is of medium height for her age, with long, brown, untidy hair, brown eyes, and a quiet, possibly shy,

145

manner. Later in the day she is to tell me of her two brothers, Peter aged 7 and James aged 4, her mum and dad and rabbit and fish. One of her favourite games is to play 'mummies and daddies' with her dolls and best friends Dawn, Susan, Tracey and Alison. At school she says she likes handwriting and tables and spellings. In other words, fairly straightforward, clear-cut tasks which make few imaginative demands.

All children enter the attractively decorated hall to the music of Grieg's *Peer Gynt* suite and settle down to enjoy the school assembly, conducted by first-year Class 3, whose spokesgirl is Tracey.

Tracey: Good morning, children.
Children: Good morning, Tracey.

After this greeting, there follows Hymn number 78 from *The Junior Hymn Book*, edited by Geoffrey Clinton (London: Hamish Hamilton, 1964), beginning:

> O Jesus, I have promised
> To serve Thee to the end;

The hymn is by John Ernest Bode, 1816–74, and number 577 in *The English Hymnal*, where two more verses are printed. These have presumably been omitted by Clinton on account of their relative unintelligibility to primary school children. However, how comprehensible the remaining verses, and the other hymns quoted in this book, are to the children who sing them is impossible to say. Certainly, no prose or poetry half so difficult would be used in the normal language lesson. In fact, Colin Harrison, of the Schools Council's *Effective Use of Reading* project (1979) has commented orally: 'The most intense and continuous reading practice in junior schools' (i.e. intensive scrutiny of the text) was to be found in assembly – for example, "Onward Christian Soldiers" – particularly if played by a Grade Three pianist.'

Yet, because of tradition, such hymns are sung each day by companies of children spanning vast age and ability ranges. The significance lies not in precise understanding, but in overall impact of the ritual, as has been indicated in previous pages in relation to other rituals.

When the hymn has been sung, Tracey politely requests: 'Please sit down for our story.' This turns out, surprisingly, to be a tale of Cowboys and Indians. Not immediately applicable to a Christian school assembly, you might think, but wait a while, and remember that Annie Oakley had a special skill which she made good use of. Not, as you might have suspected, to bump off the Indians, but rather to provide food and entertainment. In other words, Annie Oakley used her special skill for the benefit of others, and that is the theme of this morning's assembly.

The story is acted out to prove the point. Annie raises her gun in the air three times; says 'BANG!'; and each time down falls a Colonel Sanders-type stage-prop chicken. And that is without even aiming. Hence, the rashness of the three gun slingers from Class 3 who, complete with ten-gallon hats and mid-western accents, challenge Annie to a shooting competition, with various remarks of a male chauvinist nature. They are, at least, magnanimous in defeat and their leader, the ousted champion, observes: 'Young girl, you are the finest shot I've ever met.' Perhaps this is a Women's Lib tale also.

It has certainly been very carefully prepared and well acted, and has held the attention of all children and staff. The assembly is neatly rounded off, and the moral reinforced, with a prayer about the use of all gifts, and then hymn number 85 from the *Junior Hymn Book*, beginning:

> The wise may bring their learning,
> The rich may bring their wealth;

The head teacher, Mr Durham, now rises to his feet to thank the participants for their assembly efforts which were so successful. He has three further points to make. First, there is no chess report that day. Secondly, children are to be well behaved for the forthcoming Lord Mayor's visit; they are not to use the foyer doors, nor interfere with the Christmas decorations. Thirdly, they should have their collection money ready during the day for the fund to assist those recently injured in the city centre explosion.

With that, the children are dismissed and leave the hall in an orderly manner, bound for their classrooms. Lorraine's 9-year-old contemporaries, thirty-eight in all, including twenty-one girls and seventeen boys, are very well dressed and materially well cared for. They have liveliness and confidence, and some of the boys, as will be noticeable throughout the day, can hardly curb their precocity.

Their classroom is light and attractive. It is of fairly lengthy oblong shape, with one side consisting completely of windows which look on to the playground. The back wall is dominated by a big frieze of the surrounding area as it was sixty years earlier, and below this are tables of materials to delight an historian interested in primary and secondary sources: horse brasses, an old telephone, an old clock, plate, coins, old newspapers, books and pamphlets, photographs. The wall opposite the windows is largely devoted to festive decorations and has a Christmas tree, Halloween pictures and writing, as well as book reviews which, like certain hotels indicate the appropriate star rating. At the front of the class, in addition to the traditional blackboard, are four desks with odd boxes and books on them; notices concerning the panoply of mathematical signs; lists of days of the week, months of the year, numbers, monitors, etc., and a box of reading cards, one for each child. The school puts considerable stress on reading ability, and the deputy head monitors teachers' work in this area, with the intention that all children achieve as high a reading standard as possible by the time they leave. The desks in this classroom are placed neither in small groups, nor serried ranks, but in four major blocks, with about ten pupils randomly allocated to each block. So much for the physical setting.

With the exception of those in the choir, who have yet to arrive, Class 9 are now engaged in preliminary maths and reading activities as they answer in French numerals to the register called by the teacher: *'un ... deux ... trois ... quatre ... '* It is a small indication that French is taught in the school. Mr Weston, the teacher, is a man in his late 20s with beard and long hair, fashionable trousers and a blue polo neck sweater with the sleeves rolled up. He has a strong voice, cheerful manner and a pleasant, lively tone.

Lorraine is working from a maths book entitled *8 A Day*, by A. L. Griffiths (London: Oliver & Boyd, 1970). It is one of a series of maths books by Griffiths based on the system of introducing some mathematical idea (rather than concept) with an explanatory example, followed by an unvarying number of test items (for examples, *4 A Day*; *5 A Day*; *6 A Day*, and so on), designed to consolidate the original maths notion. The reprints of the series from 1970 onwards indicate extensive sales and certainly this is an approach which one commonly finds in junior schools, although the logic of it is questionable. Why 6 a day? Why not 2, if you understand what you are doing? There may be virtue in practice and consolidation, but surely medicine should be dispensed individually on the basis of a professional diagnosis?

Undeterred by such considerations, Lorraine seems to have evolved a rather idiosyncratic method of multiplication. Witness her answers, only two of which are correct:

(1)	$5 \times 2 \times 6 =$						69
(2)	$7 \times 2 \times 5 =$						70
(3)	$3 \times 4 \times 5 =$						60
(4)	$6 \times 2 \times 50 =$						59
(5)	$19 \times 5 \times 2 =$						202
(6)	$2 \times 17 \times 5 =$						38
(7)	$6 \times 3 \times 5 \times 2 =$						16
(8)	$3 \times 2 \times 5 \times 3 =$						13

This is quite disturbing. No pattern to these errors is discernible, except some possible confusion with addition. The answers seem quite arbitrary, as though Lorraine has virtually no grasp of the multiplication process. Although Mr Weston has been moving round the class from individual to individual, he has missed the stages by which Lorraine arrived at her answers. Hardly surprising in a class of thirty-eight. I missed it, too, which is more reprehensible since I am sitting next to her.

Lorraine has seemingly treated her '8 A Day' almost like prescribed tablets, the important thing being merely to take them, irrespective of the effect they might have. She is, in fact, in a mental fog, of which she is only dimly aware, and there is to be more evidence of this as the morning proceeds. She appears unable to profit from any practical concrete experience of number she might have had in earlier years. Leonard Marsh writes (1970b) that 'Children working with materials reveal that time and time again they return to simple experiences as a preliminary to extending their scheme for tackling a problem', but Lorraine appears to be bereft of appropriate strategies for solving these abstract number problems now. She stumbles like a stranger at night over a ploughed field.

Having spent seventeen minutes on the exercise, she moves to area work and the sums on the board, clearly drawn, but with no attempt at scale.

There is a fairly sustained level of conversation as work proceeds. Lorraine rarely speaks, working steadily and silently.

Mr Weston goes out with a few children to clean out the fish tank in the school foyer. The remainder continue with their work and chat, as they were doing before he left the room.

Gary I: *(to me)* How long are you going to be here?
R. M.:   Just for the day

He pulls a face, presumably to indicate that he is quite happy for me to stay. It is a kind of hospitable gesture to indicate his friendliness. He remarks that, the year before, a student had taken him for maths in a small group and that he had enjoyed it.

After six minutes the teacher returns and explains to the fish tank group that they must leave the guppies as live food for the other fish. Momentarily horrified by such impending cannibalism, the children return to the less emotive world of mathematics, but, when the choir members come in at 10.00 a.m., Alison shows that nothing has been forgotten and, using a powerful Old Testament word, tells them: 'Two little fishes are going to be sacrificed.' Simon reinforces her comment with, 'Poor innocent little guppies. He goes and kills them,' but, when questioned by Gary, 'What about your goldfish?' he laughs in such a way as to indicate that his own hands are far from clean.

From this moment on, my thoughts constantly return during the day to the fate of the guppies, as if to some friends awaiting execution. Are the children similarly concerned? Perhaps they are made of sterner stuff. Or perhaps old film personalities are paramount:

Manjit: What's Jerry Lewis going to turn into?

Gary mumbles an answer which is lost forever.

Meanwhile, Mr Weston sporadically addresses the whole class, either about the work they are doing or, less often, the noise level. He marks the '8 A Day' sums on the blackboard and the children correct their own work. Lorraine thinks she has three correct answers but, in fact, she only has two, and those, as explained earlier, appear to be attributable to pure luck or perhaps copying. She is terribly confused. She cannot find the original exercise in the book; does not ask the teacher, is baffled by the whole process, but shows few outward signs of incomprehension. Physically present, but mentally anywhere, she goes through the motions almost in a stage of amnesia. Many children, in classrooms throughout the land, must similarly disguise utter bewilderment and, in large classes, may remain undetected. If they are shy and lacking in confidence, as Lorraine appears to be, their plight is worse, for they rarely ask questions.

At 10.15a.m. a cardboard box of assorted crisps is brought in and the children descend on them as if they were gifts from the New World.

Timothy: My dad went to Margate and brought some limestone.
Simon: You're mad.
Gary: (*to Manjit*) You cheat in everything.
Manjit: (*laughing*) I don't cheat in chess.

At 10.20a.m. the class is told to put the work away.

Simon: I wonder if those two little fishes have died yet.

Another teacher, Mr Swan, comes in to talk rather movingly about the appeal mentioned in assembly by the head teacher. Mr Swan speaks of one person he knows, an apprentice, who having spent seven years in training, had a leg blown off in the explosion: 'One class has collected ninety-six pence. Can any class beat this? What sacrifice can you make? What about your biscuit money?'

For the first time this morning Lorraine speaks, very briefly, to someone else. Her best friend, Dawn, tells me: 'My dad has knocked down a wall in our house and made one room out of two. My mum wants a porch.' Dawn's concerns appear to be domestic; those of the boys relate mainly to television. Diana now approaches Lorraine: 'If you're my friend, I'm your friend.' Such emotional blackmail, implicit in the friendship equation, seems to be a popular ploy by human beings of all ages. The same phrase is used by 4-year-olds, and its adult equivalent, in negative form, seems to be: 'If you do that, Mummy won't love you any more.' Diana's overture is accepted by Lorraine with a smile and off they go for a quarter of an hour's break, after which they return to maths.

This time, they are working from what Mr Weston calls their 'ordinary maths book' (that is, *Basic Mathematics* by A. L. Griffiths,

Book 3, London: Oliver & Boyd, 1972) and he moves around the class checking the work of individuals. Such movement could be compared with the slowed-down track of the ball-bearing in a pin-ball machine. Some coils it strikes are briefly illuminated; others, struck or not, show no illumination and add nothing to the total score. The ball bearing's movement is haphazard and arbitrary; the teacher has a design and strategy. As Kant puts it in *Critique of Judgment*: the movement of the one is 'purposive', the other 'purpose-ful'. Mr Weston aims for those he missed last time round, including some who rarely show any spark. However, possibly on account of my proximity, he omits Lorraine, who appears just as bewildered as earlier.

This time she is faced with another of those cold peremptory commands often found in textbooks, which distance pupil from task: 'Find the products':

$$6 \times 4 \times 3$$
$$6 \times 4 \times 3$$
$$6 \times 4 \times 3$$

and asks me for help. I check the procedure with Dawn, just to be sure. Each horizontal line of figures is computed (i.e. total 72); the vertical line of answers is then added together (i.e. 72 + 72 + 72). Answer: 216. I explain the method to Lorraine and she manages the next one by herself:

$$9 \times 2 \times 4$$
$$9 \times 2 \times 4$$
$$9 \times 2 \times 4$$

Then, with more help from me, the next two:

$$8 \times 3 \times 5$$
$$8 \times 3 \times 5$$
$$8 \times 3 \times 5$$

| $6 \times 2 \times 10 \times 5$ | $6 \times 2 \times 10 \times 5$ | $6 \times 2 \times 10 \times 5$ |
| $6 \times 2 \times 10 \times 5$ | $6 \times 2 \times 10 \times 5$ | $6 \times 2 \times 10 \times 5$ |

Lorraine's success with these problems suggests that, had the class been smaller, she might have been able to receive the individual help she needed and could then have coped with her '8 A Day' before break.

Dawn now tries to involve me in her work, and so does Gary, with the result that I am forced to change an observational for a teaching role. It is certainly more satisfying, but it also means that the normal situation is being altered more than is inevitable anyway merely by my passive presence.

In so far as I am able to estimate the effect of my own presence, I would guess that the interference level was generally insignificant. Only in Lorraine's case does involvement loom rather larger in becoming morally inescapable. She needs individual attention from anyone on hand to give it. As for one's effect on the teacher, again this would seem largely negligible. No one can radically alter their teaching style, or the children's learning and behaviour patterns, consistently throughout a whole day. It is rather like leaving a tape recorder running; after a while you forget it is there.

The boys, meanwhile, continue their half-hearted work and whole-hearted chat: 'My brother's a sixth former' ... 'My brother goes to college' ... 'He doesn't, he doesn't.'

Timothy: My dad's going to be the referee.
Manjit: Oh God, so he has the day off.
Gary II: We're going to win. Christmas can't come. He goes to his granny's on Sunday.

The majority of primary school teachers appear now to permit such conversation while work is in progress. At its worst, it is aimless gossip which replaces or inhibits anything remotely taxing. At its best, it is a sociable activity which helps to strengthen the bonds of personal relationship and actually may enhance the quality of schoolwork. Teachers must judge for themselves when that fine dividing line is crossed.

At 11.25a.m. Mr Weston leaves the room to help prepare the fish tank for the Lord Mayor's visit. Perhaps they are to be presented to the First Citizen. Two boys, with hands on their heads, take advantage of the teacher's one-minute absence to lift their desks with their knees, as if by magic.

Upon Mr Weston's return, the children are instructed to put away their maths work and take out their local history books. All third- and fourth-year pupils are involved in a substantial project on the surrounding area which incorporates visits by and to local citizens; studies of local church and archive records, tombstones, photographs, maps, architecture; model-making; ancient craft simulation; interviews with historians, professional and amateur.

Environmental studies is capable of many different emphases – artistic, scientific, linguistic, sociological. The particular emphasis here is historical, and it is worth reminding ourselves at this stage of the potential value of an historical perspective. John Jennings (1977) summarizes seven claims which may be made. He writes:

(1) History is an important subject. It is essential to the creation of a politically articulate electorate in that it deals with the acquisition, use, abuse, and loss of power and, uniquely, shows the long-term effects of political and economic action.

(2) Secondly, through its study of remote periods and of world history, it demands the active understanding of societies with radically different assumptions from ours.

(3) Thirdly, it teaches children how to evaluate evidence to argue from incomplete evidence.

(4) Fourthly, it helps to develop children's understanding of causes and effects and of chronology.

(5) Fifthly, it is the source of a wealth of true stories – of adventure, romance, tragedy, mystery, comedy – that no child should be denied.

(6) Sixthly, it is an important element in leisure pursuits.

(7) Finally, it promotes the development of skills in narrative, description, analysis and constructive argument.

Whereas the stress on oral history in the school project would generate a wealth of material in category five, the chief justification for it would, no doubt, be found in Jennings's categories three, four and seven.[1] I revisited the school several weeks after my one-day's observation, in order to see the final exhibition of

---

1 For any teacher or student who wishes to develop or extend an environmental studies interest, the following books are recommended:

Blythe, J. (1982) *History in the Primary School* (London: McGraw Hill);
Development Education Centre (1986) *Theme Work* (Birmingham D.E.C.);
D.E.S. (1981) *Environmental Education – A Review* (London: HMSO);
Mills, D. (1987) *Teaching Geography in Primary and Middle Schools* (London: Geographical Association).

materials from this two-term local history/environmental studies team teaching enterprise. Very impressive and original it was, too, involving work by 200 pupils and six teachers.

However, perhaps at this stage it is difficult for those in the ranks to appreciate what the final outcome might be, although Gary tells me that he is enjoying the project and he proceeds to explain his own book. Lorraine has taken out hers and is labelling and colouring her bird's-eye drawing of the land. Her account of a villeinous life is given in Figure 5.1. When Mr Weston approaches and asks if she has written anything, her nod is rewarded with

A villeins life

The villeins life was very hard
In those days. they were out
side working on corn oats and fallow,
they went out evrey day
and workd hard. the Lard
of the Manor lived in the
manor House rite next to were
they were growing the corn and
that he drak ate and When
they have a feast they
play games like apple
Bobing if they play Blind
Mans But the
one wont on has to
have something over his head.
So he car t see if they
wanted there son to go to
School they have to pay.

Figure 5.1

'good', and he moves on. Gary asks her if he may borrow her light-brown pencil but, despite much cajoling, is refused.

The piece of writing by Lorraine is average, or below average, in terms of the class. The handwriting indicates some lack of co-ordination; technical competence is not yet fully developed, and sequencing is questionable. However, she has clearly been at pains to include as much information as she can, and she is able to record several facts she has learnt, either from the teacher or from reference books.

Anxious, I think, that I should see good work, Mr Weston hands me one of the best topic books, having, earlier in the day, given me 'a good maths book' to inspect. It is a natural reaction. Most of us, as teachers, have a vested interest in those who are academically successful. Perhaps because we feel they will reflect creditably upon us. Or perhaps because they are the only ones we really understand, having been academically successful ourselves. One of the best infants teachers I have ever encountered had, herself, been labelled 'remedial' at school and, to this day, has only the barest of academic qualifications. Perhaps she is so good with her children because she understands failure from within. Our academic conditioning, with its short-sighted notions of success and failure, encourages us to see the whole of life as a perpetual hurdle race.

All the children in the class are now working on a variety of tasks in their project book. Lorraine, as usual, is silent; the boys, as usual, talkative.

Manjit: Look at that scrawly writing (*that is, mine*). I can't read it.
Gary: You're not supposed to. You might write like that when you grow up. *To me*: What's that thing in your tooth?
R. M.:   It's a gold filling.

Three or four children leer around me with open mouths, showing me their fillings. Their interest is not of the detached scientific variety which I tried to describe in 7-year-old David's dinner-table group. It seems more like the diversionary tactical kind, designed to replace work. My filling has now figured in two chapters of this book and, lest any reader has a mental image of some grotesque monstrous obtrusion, I should point out that it is a perfectly ordinary, small, National Health, gold piece, only noticeable by its position between my two front teeth.

For several minutes, Lorraine has been sitting, sucking her biro and writing the odd word. 'How much did you copy of mine?' asks Dawn. No answer, but I think it was quite a bit. Lorraine takes her work to Mr Weston, who corrects some of her spellings. He then announces a reprieve for the guppies. They are to be placed in a jar on the radiator and the children may look at them so long as they do not knock them over. The announcement brings sighs of relief that only such an eleventh-hour pardon could provoke. Lorraine looks up and listens to the news, but her thoughts remain hidden.

It is 11.55a.m. and the boys and girls are told to clear away their books and wait for the bell. As they sit with arms folded, Mr Weston takes advantage of the spare time for some mental arithmetic.

Mr W.:   Eight fours, Andrew.
Andrew: Thirty-two.
Mr W.:   Stand by the door. Marilyn, seven sixes.
Marilyn: Forty-two.
Mr W.:   Stand by the door.

Children who answer correctly are allowed to line up; others wait in their seats. Early escape is the reward for a right response, rather like remission of sentence for good conduct.

At 12.10p.m. three children only are left in the classroom. Simon is washing out in the sink the gravel from the fish tank; Shirley has ear-ache and remains in to keep warm; Lorraine has just tape recorded a short conversation with me. She felt that she had had 'quite a good morning', and had enjoyed doing the area shapes from the blackboard, as well as the reading, writing and tables. In the afternoon she was anticipating 'craft or anything'. Her speech is quiet and hesitant and its content thin. When asked what she watched on television, she replied, 'Cartoons. Comedies. I can't remember anything else'. Manjit, Gary, Timothy and Co. would have been garrulous, if not eloquent, on such a subject. Undoubtedly, Lorraine is quite talkative with her girl-friends when they are playing together. To be tape recorded by a comparative stranger must be a fairly taxing experience for her.

Afternoon school begins at 1.30 p.m. but, twenty minutes before this, a number of boys and girls are in the classroom, preparing it for craft by putting coverings over the desks, and paint brushes and water in strategic spots. David asks me: 'You're a script writer, aren't you?' and, possibly echoing Manjit's earlier words, Lorraine adds, 'A scribble writer', and laughs. Her confidence appears to be increasing.

When the bell sounds the rest of the children return in ones and twos. Manjit enters singing a pop song: 'The girls grab the boys and they go wild, wild, wild'. Mr Weston is, significantly, not far behind.

Mr W.:   Quickly sit down, please ... Can we have everyone sitting down, boys, please? ... Right, erm. Can we have everyone sitting down then? Right erm. Register then ... I'm still waiting ...

It is a small comment rich, in what have been called teachers' *focus* words (that is, *right ... erm ... please ... then ...*). Notice, too the pedagogic pseudo-questions, designed to promote classroom order, and the reliance on shared assumptions between teacher and pupils.

Soon there is silence.

Mr W.:   Can you clear this mess up that you made this morning? ... Right ... erm ... Girls?
Girls: *Un ... deux ... trois ... quatre ...*

There is a periodic investigation of the whereabouts of those whose French numbers are not called out, during which time Lorraine is involved in cleaning out parts of the sink, a job she obviously enjoys.

Mr W.:   Boys?
Boys: *Un ... deux ... trois ... quatre ...* (Once again, *onze*, comes out as *awze*)
Mr W.:   Right. Hands on your head, everyone.

Immediate silence enables Mr Weston to give further instructions. Children will be involved in activities relating to Christmas. Choice and variety are now permitted, whereas neither was allowed during the morning session. Some will finish their Christmas cards, either working singly or in pairs. Some will be working

158

on large pieces of card to produce a Biblical scene, which will ultimately decorate the windows. Its subject will either be the stable scene; the three kings; the shepherds and the angel; or those following the star.

Susan: Who was following the star?
Manjit: The three kings, stupid.

This leads into a question and answer session between teacher and children regarding the details of the Biblical birth narratives. Lorraine sits quietly, staring down at the table, and then, looking around at those children who answer, she whispers one response to herself – 'the lambs'– and puts up her hand to answer, but is not asked.

The discussion over, most children settle to their various tasks. Lorraine is not clear what to do and goes out to ask for guidance. Mr Weston offers her a piece of paper but she rejects it and elects to work with Dawn and another girl on their Christmas card. The three girls stand around this picture of a colourful and attractive, if lop-sided, rabbit, about 60 by 45 centimetres, each painting a part of it, before moving on to produce multi-coloured patches around the rabbit by dabbing with small sponges. There is a little conversation between the other two girls, but Lorraine is generally quiet, although fully accepted as a member of the trio.

All the children in the class are now actively involved on different tasks, either working alone or in pairs or small groups. Some are producing a nativity scene motif for the window decoration. Others are engaged in elaborating on single letters from the word CHRISTMAS (for example, a Father Christmas with a 60 centimetre high 'S' around him). Others are carefully designing cards.

As they are thus engaged, so they adopt a variety of comfortable positions in which to work. Some paint standing up; others sitting down; a few lying on the floor. Some can concentrate for long periods of time, Manjit, for example, who did little work of a non-oral variety this morning, is absolutely silent for half an hour, completely absorbed in his own nativity scene.

Lorraine, on the other hand, is not so involved and moves regularly from painting to sink, now sponging paint from her skirt, now cleaning out her saucer and fish-paste jar. When she paints it seems that she invariably goes over parts already covered, or touches up parts here and there, rather than risk anything new.

More often, she leaves her little group and moves around the room, or into the corridor to look at the decorations, telling me *en route* that she does not want to do any more on the rabbit. She shows particular interest in a painting of 'MERRY CHRISTMAS' in glistening letters (made by sprinkling glitter particles over newly painted letters and then shaking off the loose bits). Then she hovers in the doorway, sometimes sucking her thumb sometimes hopping from one foot to another, looking like an attractive little waif. Such free-wheeling sessions seem to be important to some children and cannot always be contained within normal break periods. Conversely, optimum learning and concentration periods come not to order. Like telephone calls, they are unanticipated and of varying duration.

All this time, Mr Weston has been a peripatetic adviser, going round giving help; distributing paint and paper; relaying information regarding the whereabouts of other materials; asking why so many children are round the sink; holding up a painting to establish its ownership.

At 2.34p.m. he announces, 'Time to pack up', and begins to distribute clearing-up jobs. Children move in all directions, like a snooker formation struck by the cue ball, collecting paintings to hang up for drying, washing out brushes and pots, replacing scissors and pencils. Such regular tidying up is a constant feature of classroom life and it needs to be done efficiently and smoothly, as it is here. Lorraine is asked to pick up some pieces of paper from the floor and this she does, slowly and meticulously, chasing minute scraps with brush and pan. Nine children are flushed out of the stockroom; two or three settle down with reading books; Dawn tells me that her dog always jumps on her bed in the morning to wake her up for school. It is an odd, irrelevant, inconsequential comment and therefore, perhaps worth recording.

At 2.45p.m., when the bell sounds, girls and boys line up in separate rows by the door. It must be second nature for many teachers to distinguish between their pupils in this way but, administrative convenience aside, one wonders if there is much to be said for it. Emphasizing sexual identity, as is done many times within the ritual of many a school day, does not seem to have much point.

Lorraine, however, is in neither line. Instead, she is concentrating on hunting for bits of rubbish. Like many pupils, she clearly enjoys tidying up. She steps in the bin to stamp down for more space, gets her foot stuck and falls over. It is almost the classic clown ploy here performed artlessly. Only after two exhortations from the teacher is Lorraine persuaded to leave her job and follow her peers into the playground.

After a quarter of an hour's break, all have returned and, on hearing Mr Weston's words, 'Pencils out, please', the word goes round in a whisper, 'Spelling ... Spelling'. It is, indeed, and the test commences. As is customary in this kind of game, single-word test items are generally put within the context of a simple sentence, or a brief discussion. In some cases, the isolated word gives rise to a short language lesson. Unlike Lucy's spelling test in Chapter 4, the words here have either been selected quite arbitrarily, or to reflect children's individual errors in the past few days. Here are the items:

(1)	*mountain*	(Mr W.:	Give me a sentence with the word 'mountain' in it.
		Pupil:	The mountain is very tall.
		Mr W.:	High, not tall. What's the name of the tallest mountain?
(2)	*newspaper*	(A short discussion ensues about local and national newspapers.)	
(3)	*middle*	(Timothy:	Johnny threw a dart in the middle of the board.)
(4)	*curtain*	(Mr W.:	For every curtain in this room, the girls made a press-stud button.)
(5)	*playmate*	(Julie:	My playmate always makes friends with me.)
(6)	*settle*		
(7)	*extra*	(Mr W.:	The newsman shouted, 'Extra, Extra! Read all about it!' In the discussion which follows, the link with number two is developed.)
(8)	*meddle*	(Mr W.:	'Don't meddle in anyone else's affairs' said the wise old man.)
(9)	*fountain*	(Jacqueline achieves rhythm, if not sense, with: 'There was a fountain on top of the mountain.) *(The children laugh)*.	
(10)	*paddle*	(Mr W.:	A canoe has one paddle.
		Andrew:	The steamer had a big paddle.)

(11) *platform*   (Mr W.:   The train is about to enter at platform six.

                        Alison: Mr and Mrs Brown met Padding-
ton on Paddington Station's plat-
form.)

(12) *honest*   (Pupil: My sister isn't very honest.)

Lorraine has all the words correct except the first, which she wrote as *moutain*. The children mark their own spellings, as is the custom, and then hand in their books for later rechecking by the teacher.

Lorraine's spelling test did not generate the same degree of heightened emotion as occurred in Lucy's class, where the atmosphere was almost hysterical. Yet it was conducted as a serious activity, and in such a context that the children knew that something important was happening. It was, in military terms, the equivalent of a major kit inspection, rather than routine checking of equipment and, because of that, it carried with it the associated feelings of unnaturalness and tension. Without minimizing the significance of the importance of spelling (and without over-emphasizing it either), it does seem that a better standard might be obtained by a more natural approach, placing it within the context of normal on-going work and investigation. It could become, to use Bullock's (1975) words, 'part of the fabric of normal classroom experience, neither dominating nor neglected' (para. 11.14)

In this respect, I find the list of 'handy hints' produced by Mike Torbe (1977) very helpful and, with his kind permission, would like to quote them now. He makes ten points.

(1) Teaching from spelling lists, on the basis of study followed by tests, does not help the child to become an efficient speller in his writing.

(2) Slightly better is to use the test followed by study of the words spelled incorrectly; but this causes only a marginal improvement.

(3) Spelling rules are of little help, because if they are thorough enough to explain a pattern, they're likely to be incomprehensible to the children.

(4) Children who have a good general understanding of sound-symbol relationship, even if they do not spell well at the

moment, are, as Margaret Peters says, 'well on their way' to becoming good spellers.

(5) Teachers who have an enthusiasm and enjoyment for spoken and written language, and a care for it, have pupils who are likely to be good spellers.

(6) An interest in words, their meanings, shapes, history and sound, generates improved spelling.

(7) The more interested pupils are in what they write, the more attention they are prepared to give to its appearance, including spelling.

(8) When children recognize that their writing is for a real public audience, not just the teacher but other people, they are more likely to be concerned with their spelling.

(9) Good spelling habits are:
– The habit of checking guesses by looking the word up, or asking.
– The habit of proof-reading.
– The habit of spelling analysis: How is it pronounced? Is the spelling phonetic? How can I remember the difficult bits?

(10) Spelling is changing all the time, but slowly. What one generation finds appalling, the next generation accepts ...
... Be careful, therefore, about condemning words too quickly ... Give your time not to outraged attacks on what offends you, but on the more urgent and useful task of teaching pupils how to spell by considering the recurring patterns of English spelling.

Perhaps such an approach, designed to take the heat and unnaturalness out of teaching spelling, while probably rendering it more effective also, should be welcomed. But old habits, like old soldiers, die hard.

The test done, Lorraine and her classmates now read their fiction books for a few moments, anticipating a singing lesson. However, when Mr Weston returns from his fruitless search for a tape recorder, he informs them that they will finish the day with reading. It is 3.30p.m. on a Friday and the children are restless.

Gary informs me that his book has got bare pictures in it, and so it has, showing young children having a shower and a bath. The boys and girls nearby laugh at Gary's words and I imagine his book is quite popular, if only for its visual element. The word *bare* seem to be a particularly rude one for young children.

I ask Lorraine about her library book (*A Dog and Two Red Heads*, by Jan Macdonald, London: Harrap, 1959) and she tells me, 'It's all right'. The jacket blurb informs us that the book is about an orphan from Glasgow who goes to live with his grandparents in Morayshire. Lorraine has the book open in front of her but is not interested in it. There is more attraction in the jokes and comments of those about her.

Manjit: Are you a C.M.?
Simon: Why?
Manjit: If you were, you'd be a sex maniac.
Simon: Did you hear that joke about the Irish mastermind? He was asked, 'What's your name?' ... 'Pass'.
Gary: Why did the Irish road sweeper break his leg when sweeping leaves? ... He fell off the tree.

It is the season of mists and Irish jokes, and even Debbie is emboldened to ask me a riddle, albeit not an Irish one: 'What did the big chimney say to the little chimney?' I feign ignorance, but her answer is not what I expect or understand: 'You're too young to ring'.

At 3.45p.m. Mr Weston calls all children to order and they prepare to listen to him read a story from *It Must Be Magic* by Miriam Huber and Frank Salisbury (Herts: Nisbet, 1962). It is, in fact a Grimm fairy tale of a mouse, a donkey and a bear, to which the class pays reasonable attention. Lorraine concentrates particularly hard, following the narrative closely in her copy of the book. After five minutes the errant tape recorder is brought in but rejected at this late stage in the day.

A minute before 4.00p.m. the children are instructed to line up by the door in their separate ranks. The teacher says: 'It's definitely the girls' (that is, the boys are moving) ... 'Now it's the boys' (that is, the girls are moving). When the bell sounds, the girls are allowed off first, to a small cheer.

Sequel 1   School Assemblies

We have seen in earlier chapters that the school assembly, often the first and only corporate experience of the day for all children, can have considerable power. In Rashda's case (Chapter 2), the stress fell on reinforcement of the school as a caring community. This was true also of David's assembly (Chapter 3) which, in addition, highlighted the significance of the individual within the group, via the impressive birthday-boy ritual. Lucy's Roman Catholic school (Chapter 4) could assume a reasonable degree of acceptance of one particular Christian stance, and therefore could hold a full-scale mass for pupils, teachers and parents. In this instance, there was a community of faith in which worship was not inappropriate.

However, in a pluralist society, and in a school where education should 'scrutinize' rather than 'assume' belief (Hull, 1975), the school assembly, mandatory since the 1944 Education Act, becomes highly questionable unless it can be justified on social and/or curriculum grounds.

Rachel Gregory in her book, *Assemblies*, which is part of the Bedforshire RE Series (1985), provides a clear and concise discussion of this issue. She also includes some very practical suggestions about the organization of assemblies in schools and outlines a range of content that can be explored in appropriate ways through assemblies.

In this brief extract from her book she discusses ways in which worship may be a part of school assemblies without appearing to undermine some basic democratic and educational principles deemed to be appropriate in a pluralist society.

Why Assembly?

The legal requirement is not the sole reason for schools having assembly. Most schools have assembly because they believe it can be a worthwhile educational activity which adds something of value to the life of the school.

A school is a community and assembly is an important time of 'coming together'. It is an occasion which helps to foster a sense of belonging. Of course it is not essential to see a community physically gathered together in order to feel part of it, but that experience of a community may help younger children to a greater understanding of less tangible communities like neighbourhood, faith-community, world family.

It is a time for the school community to affirm and celebrate the ideals and values it cares about, and to reflect individual and group experiences which help to develop these ideals.

However, the need to foster community spirit and to draw attention to shared values could be met by a purely secular assembly, so what is the place of worship?

What About Worship?

The Education Act says the purpose of coming together is *worship*. But if this means a closed approach which assumes that those present hold particular beliefs, then it could be regarded, in many cases, as an infringement of individual integrity and inappropriate in the school context.

However, it does not necessarily follow that worship should be abandoned in school assembly. Teachers have a professional responsibility to introduce pupils to various different areas of experience including the spiritual – and the spiritual dimension surely includes some experience and understanding of worship. The HMI Working Paper 'Curriculum 11–16' (1977) identifies the following areas of experience: aesthetic or creative, ethical, linguistic, mathematical, physical, scientific, social and political, and spiritual.

If we want to retain worship as an essential area of experience but also respect the integrity of those participating, we must take a fresh look at our definition of 'worship'. The Education Act needs to be reinterpreted in the light of present day social and educational conditions so that an assembly-for-worship makes educational sense for the 1980s.

What is worship? The Education Act does not state that the worship should be Christian – that was taken for granted. However, the lack of specification clearly permits a broader definition.

166

It is also interesting to note that the Act uses the word 'collective' rather than 'corporate' to describe worship. This provides scope for a variety of responses by those present, whereas in a corporate activity all participate in the same manner.

One way forward is to go for a *broader definition* of the word 'worship'. Worship can be defined as having to do with 'worth'. It would be concerned with identifying, affirming and celebrating certain ideals and values held to be of central importance to the community which worships.

This is a useful definition as it accommodates a variety of practices. The danger underlying this definition is that assembly could degenerate into a gathering concerned with upholding school rules and implanting a moral code.

Perhaps it is not a new definition of 'worship' that is needed, but a *broader understanding* of 'worship' in the traditional sense. This would involve thinking of worship as a basic human activity, in which everyone shares in their own way. Not worship as practised by any particular faith, but rather focussing on aspects of worship in which all can participate: wonder, awe, mystery, celebration, reverence, fellowship, awareness. Assembly is a time to share in the deeper levels of ordinary experience.

Assembly can be more than a secular activity. Where worship is understood in a broad sense, assembly can be an activity that:

- fosters a sense of fellowship by bringing pupils together;
- brings pupils to the threshold of worship;
- creates an atmosphere in which those who wish to worship can do so;
- encourages a reflective approach to life;
- increases sensitivity so that pupils are more aware of the search for meaning in the face of life's mysteries;
- introduces pupils to aspects of religious worship in an open and honest atmosphere;
- encourages pupils to express their responses in a variety of different ways: music, dance, drama, movement, art and craft, poetry and prose.

If school assembly is not an explicit act of worship but an enjoyable educational experience, closely integrated with the life and work of the school, focussing on what is of 'worth', and being aware of some of the vital elements of worship, then the

167

problem of the two opposing requirements – educational and legal – can be reconciled. If worship is understood in this broad sense it has a right and proper place in school assembly.

References

Gregory R. (1985) *Assembly* (Bedfordshire Education Service, Bedford: Bedfordshire RE Services).
Hull, J. (1975) *School Worship: An Obituary* (London: SCM).
For a regular supply of practical suggestions relating to school assemblies, the CEM magazine, *Assembly File* is highly recommended.

Sequel 2 Maths Teaching

It was fairly evident in Chapter 5 that Lorraine's grip on certain mathematical processes and concepts was quite tenuous. When given individual help she could achieve some success, but, left to her own devices, she floundered. The vast majority of primary schools, according to the Cockcroft Report (1983) spend a good deal of time on maths teaching, but what actually occurs during that time is clearly of greater significance. Lorna Ridgway (1976) outlines her criteria for good maths teaching and good maths learning and, with her kind permission, I should like to quote the nine points she makes.

(1) Since the ultimate capacity to think abstractly does not origi-nate in abstract teaching but depends upon the learner's own interaction with the external world in thought-provoking situations, the teacher's responsibility is to provide for the appropriate mathematical activity in breadth and in depth.

(2) Children proceed along a broad front; a variety of numerical and mathematical ideas at approximately the same level is provided.

(3) All pupils need not necessarily go through all processes in the same order.

(4) The programme is so arranged that learners return fre-quently to the same aspect of mathematics to renew their grasp and deepen understanding.

(5) Recording of number and mathematical experience often takes forms other than the numerical. Young children grasp and use number ideas expressed in pictures, diagrams, charts, graphs, histograms, mapping and three dimensional structures and use them more effectively than they did the former purely computational '*sums*'.

(6) Apparatus, text-books and task assignments are used flexibly as learning aids; at any level their use may be modified, dispensed with or prolonged as necessary.

(7)   Mechanical mastery dependent upon rote-learning has a very limited place: it is not usually undertaken unless the process it represents is fully understood: but the terms required to express mathematical ideas are memorized through constant use and this memorization may occasionally be tested.

(8)   Individual interest is highly valued: children may prolong their work in an area that interests them even if other aspects or subjects are temporarily neglected.

(9)   Much help is available to the teacher. Commercially produced equipment abounds, from beads and bricks to the structural materials of Cuisenaire rods, Stern or Dienes blocks, Logiblocs, metrication kits, Poleidoblocs and calculators and computers. The literature is rich, ranging from theoretical studies ... to practical guidance.

Commercial assignment-card kits make individual work comparatively easy, although there is often need to use them selectively.

Sequel 3   Teacher Training Tasks

Chapter 5 Lorraine

(1)   How does Lorraine's assembly match the points made in the Sequel on 'School Assemblies?'

(2)   What seem to be the characteristics of the atmosphere in Lorraine's class?

(3)   How do you distinguish between social chat in class and discussion about work? At what point does the former become worrying?

(4)   What signs of confusion and ignorance does Lorraine show during her day? How do you, with a large class, attempt to monitor such confusion with each of your boys and girls?

(5)   How do Lorraine's apparent needs differ from Manjit's? In what ways would you try to meet both sets of needs?

(6)   What are the advantages and disadvantages of such regular activities as '8 a Day?' Measure your views against those of Lorna Ridgway in her Sequel on 'Maths Teaching'.

(7)   Part of Lorraine's day is occupied in topic work based on her school environment. Working with a colleague or in a small group, select a theme or topic appropriate for the age and ability range of your children, and prepare a collection of suitable prose extracts; short stories; poetry; drama possibilities; library research tasks; pictures; objects; tapes etc. with assignments of all kinds. Your main objective would be to produce a box of stimulus material on the chosen topic.

(8)   Suppose Lucy (Chapter 4) and Lorraine (Chapter 5) swopped schools. On the basis of the evidence presented here, how might the differing atmospheres and curriculum styles affect each of them?

Chapter 6

Peter, Aged 10

I do some more Reading Lab if I get the chance

The School

Peter's school opened in 1974 and is likely to remain fairly small with some 160 children, three classes of infants on the ground floor and four of juniors upstairs. Serving an area of small mid–1930s owner-occupier semi-detached houses and new council town houses, the school, which is tucked away at the end of a cul-de-sac, initially took in a disproportionate number of children with behavioural problems. Some were from the nearby children's home, and others had either been advised or required to leave the schools they had previously been attending. Perhaps any new school, like a New Year's resolution, offers promise to those who have previously failed, or been unhappy, or been declared redundant.

Near the attractive building is a brook, a small bank with mature trees, a sunken wall, a pond which was previously a rubbish dump, and a scrap metal yard. In other words, sources of considerable interest to any school keen on environmental studies, as this one is.

There are seven full-time teachers including the head, who spends most of his day around the school in classrooms or working with individual children, two part-timers for needle-work and special needs attention, and a nursery assistant. Parents often come in to help with practical activities, particularly cooking.

The day

It is 9.00a.m. on Monday morning, a dull day with rain on the wind. Sixteen or so children are grouped like molecules in small clusters of three or four in an open-plan-style classroom. All appear to be healthy and well cared for and quite smartly dressed in colourful clothes. There is an element of vertical grouping as the class, numbering some thirty-two, contains 9- to 11-year olds. This includes thirteen boys, one of whom is, reportedly, a kleptomaniac receiving psychiatric attention. Some of the girls showing signs of fashion consciousness are wearing modern-style shoes and have the remains of nail varnish on their fingers.

Peter is in one of the groups, a tallish boy with fairly long curly hair, spectacles, and a brace on his teeth. Brace apart, he is rather like the stereotype of the scientist in embryo. There is no school uniform and he is dressed in tweed trousers, a purple shirt, a dark-red baggy jumper and brown shoes.

The classroom is as attractive and colourful as a miniature department store at sale time. Different parts are set aside for different activities, although dividing lines are by no means hard and fast. The practical area has a functional appearance, with tiled floor, sink, work surfaces, pottery wheel, clay, paints. The reading corner offers another image, with a carpeted area, easy chairs and cushions, a switched-on bedside table lamp, and displayed books of all kinds. Elsewhere, two caged gerbils run about in sight of a model of the Golden Gate Bridge, San Francisco. Mobiles and plastic shapes hang from the ceiling girders. The walls and windows are covered with evidence of what the children have recently been working on. There are paintings, collages and pieces of writing about fire. Graphs indicate that the three most popular daily newspapers for parents are the *Sun*, *Mirror*, and the local evening paper. (One teacher whom I know, from another school, is astute enough to verify such results as these, obtained from the children, by records of sales from every local newsagent within his catchment area.) The most popular children's comic is *The Beano*.

In addition to the graphs, there are colour prints which show scenes from the school youth hostel trip to Ludlow. An ordnance survey map pinpoints the school in its surroundings. There are twigs, branches, pottery, embroidery, prints, paintings, trays, boxes, fabric, an old boot, as well as charts, posters and more conventional classroom paraphernalia.

This classroom is a treasure house whose message is the same as Howard Carter's to Lord Carnarvon on discovering Tutenkhamen's tomb. When asked, 'Can you see anything?' he replied stammeringly, 'Yes, wonderful things'. Every boy and girl can find something of interest in this room. Even so, few teachers would entirely support the assertion of John Dewey (1966), tantalizing as it is: 'The only way in which adults can consciously control the kind of education which the immature can get, is by controlling the environment in which they act, and hence think and feel.' As Dearden questions (1968): 'Which environment is THE environment or the one that is to be stimulating, or structured? Can one literally PROVIDE experiences?' Perhaps not, but few children, I imagine, would happily exchange this room for one with completely bare walls and bleak brown desks. The difference is that between a personalized, attractive bedroom, and a solitary confinement cell.

The boys and girls, by now up to their full complement, are standing or sitting, waiting for their teacher, who is also deputy head, delayed with a parent. (In fact, this turned out to be Peter's father, who had come to discuss the secondary school his son should move to at the beginning of the next academic year, and who was the first parent to broach the matter at this stage.)

Mr Barnes, the teacher, enters. He is a tallish, bearded man in his early 30s, dressed in a brown suit, purple shirt and yellowish tie. He is quietly spoken, with a gentle but firm manner. It is not without significance that he taught these children the previous year also. Straight away he is surrounded by a group of them who appear to have brought him cellophane bags containing small black sponges. These are, in fact, coals for the enventual launching of their hot-air balloon. Almost by way of reciprocation for their gifts, Mr Barnes hands out individual white folders to each child. Peter's, with his name on it, contains material from the SRA scheme which we have encountered in previous chapters. Amongst other papers, he has a green Power Builder Progress Chart and a pink Rate Builder Progress Chart. Who could fail to be impressed by the promise of such dynamism and energy, even if they are only comprehension exercises?

Peter elects not to work in his own classroom and goes next door to the tiny library, a room lined with shelves and containing a television, a spirit duplicator, a Polaroid camera, a slide projector, and other pieces of audio-visual equipment, all within easy reach of any child. The school trusts its older pupils not only to work on their own, but to do so near valuable equipment, if they wish. This is something which Peter particularly appreciates, as he will indicate later.

There are four chairs around the table in the library and a few cushions on the floor, to suit all sedentary tastes. Two other children are reading in the library as Peter collects his SRA card from the box and immediately settles down to work on the short prose piece, *Junks of the Yangtze*, by Anne Terry White (2 Purple, Lab. 11a).

The story is written in a dramatic tradition, designed to appeal to juniors with a taste for adventure and proximity, through literature, to danger. One notices the use of the present tense, with regular elisions ('isn't', 'it's'. 'that's'); the numerous exclamation marks and question marks; the short sharp sentences; and the rhetorical flourishes ('He was born on a junk'; 'He will die on a junk'). Multiple-choice questions are so designed as to check a child's reading of the lines, between the lines and beyond the lines. Items in the vocabulary section are based on words in the prose story, and thus there is something of a marriage between the piece of fictional/factual reading and the grammar exercises.

After three minutes of work, Peter is called back to the classroom to pay his dinner money, a traditional Monday morning ritual, and sits chatting with two of his friends. Others are doing the same while they await their turn. Some chat about television programmes. Some read their books.

Since the head teacher is out of school collecting equipment, Mr Barnes has additional duties and is again occupied with a parent for ten minutes. On his return he walks round with his register. Whether he is absent or present, there is no perceptible change in the children's behaviour as they read, chat, write. All are actively and sensibly engaged. It is a pattern which will remain constant throughout the day until PE and the story. Such is the organization, as will be made clear shortly, that the teacher is freed to become a peripatetic adviser, working with individual children, rather than remaining the dominant focal point of the room.

Mr Barnes now speaks very, very quietly and asks all children to close their books and listen to what he has to say. He wishes to see Group 1 first in the English corner, with their English and maths books. Group 3 will find their week's work detailed in the maths corner. Group 2 have finished their graphs and all have been handed in except Veronica's and that is now ready. They will try another graph this week, different from those of last week and perhaps involving surveys on spending money or bed times.

The issue of grouping for learning is one which every school and class teacher must come to terms with. Age and/or ability are the most common criteria used. Age groupings would be either *chronological*, (that is, complete classes of more or less the same age) or *vertical* (that is, children of varying ages within the same class). Ability groupings would be formed either by *streaming* (that is, children of similar attainment in the same class) or by *unstreaming* (that is, mixed-ability classes, either by design or arrived at in a random manner) or, in a large school, by *banding* (that is, a hierarchy of two or three bands, say A, B, C, with children of varying ability within each band. In theory, all Band A children would have an academic attainment higher than all Band B, and so on). In addition to these methods of grouping, there is also *team teaching*, which may cut across any of the groupings just mentioned. In this instance, a team of two or more teachers is responsible for two or more classes.

Whatever the overall system of school grouping, each teacher needs to decide the most appropriate way in which to organize children within the classroom. Sometimes the class will be taught as a unit, and this is appropriate where a body of information is to be conveyed or a process explained. Sometimes there will be individual or pair work. Often there will be group work, as in Peter's class at this moment. The advantages of such a group approach are clear. Facilities and materials, often in short supply, may be more economically used; the problems of classroom management may be eased; a measure of choice, either of content and/or sequence, may be permitted; social interaction can occur and a natural working relationship develop; the talents of a number of children may be enlisted and combined. It all depends on the task in hand. The ideal is to ring the changes on these different methods of grouping, choosing whatever is appropriate for whatever activity, so that children may experience the social, linguistic and academic demands and benefits of each.

Mr Barnes reminds his class of a check list of activities which he has written on the blackboard and which need to be covered by everyone at some time during the week. The time tabling of the work is left to the children. This might be termed by some an example of the 'integrated' or 'undifferentiated'. Strictly speaking, it is neither. 'Flexible week' might be a better term, since the sequencing of the work is a matter for the children, provided that all tasks are completed by Friday.

These tasks include, as the blackboard indicates, SRA; mathematics; *Sound Sense* (that is, a book of language exercises by A. E. Tansley); word games; handwriting; reading; Batik tie and dye; science; new books. The teacher has also provided a clip board with a list of names on it of boys and girls he wishes to hear read, either that day or the day after. When they have read to him they can cross their names off the list. The tie and dye group needs to try again since the dye did not take too well previously. Equipment for the science experiments is in the practical work area.

Clearly, such a flexible mode of organization requires considerable planning by the teacher before school starts. The structure may be unobtrusive but there is no doubt of its existence. Just such a point was made by Bennett (1976) in his research into the relationship between 'teaching styles and pupil progress'. His results indicated quite unequivocally that formal methods of teaching (which he carefully defined) were linked with a greater measure of progress in the basic skills (also defined). However, there was one case observed of a 'High Gain Informal Classroom' and, about this, he wrote as follows:

> The teacher was a woman in her middle thirties with ten years' teaching experience. The school was situated in a new town and the class, according to the teacher, comprised pupils with the full range of abilities ... The curriculum emphasis was placed on the cognitive rather than the affective/aesthetic. Standards were set by the head ... The teacher had her own system of records, mainly of attainment, including records of group and individual work, and also of social behaviour. She had also built up a large stock of teaching materials over the years. With reference to incentives, she stated that she was the main incentive ... In the context of open-plan primary schools it has been said by practitioners and advisers alike that successful implementation requires good organisation and a clear structure. This would seem to be exemplified in this classroom. Although the classroom was evidently orientated towards informal practices, the content of the curriculum was clearly organised and well structured.

The same, however, could be said of Mr Barnes's classroom and curriculum.

At 9.40a.m. he calls for Group 1 which moves, as do the others, to action stations. Peter returns to the small library room and immediately settles down to his SRA work alongside six or seven other children, including five from his own class. He works steadily and thoroughly, occasionally speaking to his friend Kevin (for example, about sharpening his pencil) or listening to him (for example, about a query on his work card). In other words, comments related to the work in hand.

A social scientist in the making comes in to ask about pocket money. 'What pocket money do you have on school days?' she says. One of the boys claims to receive 50p a day, but this is hotly disputed by his friends (or creditors). Peter answers, 'Thirty-five. No. Forty-five', and the statistic is duly recorded for the graph which Veronica is producing.

The construction of graphs based on real up-to-date information, has more than intrinsic interest. It gives children an opportunity to exercise certain social skills in the acquiring of information – that is, they often work together, interviewing both friends and strangers. It gives them the opportunity first to record information in a relevant context and then to evaluate it – that is, to develop powers of discrimination. It allows them to exercise mathematical and language skills – that is, in the presentation of their findings. Above all, since a visual medium is often more accessible to more people, the graph is a modern means of conveying information and one which children will meet constantly in later life, particularly on television and computer programmes.

Kevin now checks his SRA answers and is loudly accused by Peter of copying them from the answer card. Claims and counter-claims are heard. The two boys discuss their answers as another teacher comes in to work with one of her children. Such one-to-one correspondence is frequent in this semi-open-plan setting, with children engaged in a variety of tasks and having the freedom not only to choose the sequence of those tasks and, in many cases, the tasks themselves, but also their place of working. All the classroom doors along the corridor are open and one can hear the subdued sounds of talking, walking (that is, some of the children are measuring the corridor), and moving of chairs. Boys and girls are constantly coming into the library for a variety of purposes; many to use the reference books; some to take off the hook a rubber with a large tab attached to it which proclaims emphatically: I AM AN ENGLISH RUBBER.

This tab performs the same function as those enormous plastic slabs attached to hotel keys; it makes them more difficult to lose or overlook. As such, it is a small reminder of the organizational skills needed in any classroom, but particularly one where children are encouraged to move around a good deal. Lorna Ridgway (1976) offers a useful list of 'aids to good housekeeping in the classroom'. Most of these nine points are observed by Mr Barnes and his colleagues.

(1) A clear indication of the location of task-areas and their appropriate material.
(2) Labels on the outside of boxes, packages and tins.
(3) Notices on cupboards and shelves stating the contents.
(4) Colour-coding on the backs of jigsaws and all similar equipment.
(5) Grading systems by colour or number indicating levels of difficulty in task-cards, text-books and apparatus.
(6) Plenty of hooks within the children's reach for aprons, brushes and cloths, wall pockets and bags.
(7) Printed statements of simple job-analysis (e.g. the best way to clean out the guinea-pig cage.
(8) Indexing of books, at first in the book-corner by colour code or other simple classification, then, in the main library by the selected school system.
(9) Indexing of the resource centre.

It is now 10.02a.m. and Peter is still working quietly and steadily. One minute later he goes in search of the SRA check card saying, 'Out the way!' to one of the nearby girls. Within context the command is less rude and less brusque than it might seem in print.

Peter has all but one of his thirty-two answers correct; Kevin has seven wrong. For a moment or so the two boys discuss who is the brainier as they compare their scores on the gold, purple and orange cards. The school itself appears neither to promote nor discourage academic competition and its neutral stance has the effect of focusing attention on the task. But, individually, children compare themselves with each other and, with such a highly structured hierarchical scheme as SRA, could scarcely avoid doing so.

When he has completed two more purple cards, Peter will move on to rose. He visits his classroom for a moment before returning to register his success on his record card. Meanwhile, Kevin reads aloud from his new card a passage entitled, *The Methodical Composer* (Gold 2, Lab. IIa), about a man's meticulous habits of eating daily fifty strands of spaghetti, each thirty centimetres in length. Peter chuckles at the story but then says, 'Can you read in your mind?' For a moment or so Kevin proves he can, but soon returns to his preference for reading aloud.

Peter now delves into the SRA box, as a secretary might into a filing cabinet. 'You're mad if you can't do orange', he says to the girl nearby and produces for himself a purple card (Purple 10, Lab. IIa) with a prose piece called, *Treasure Trove* by Bill Beatty. Unlike Kevin, who is still declaiming to anyone within hearing distance, he reads his card silently. Then, for a moment, a small group of children discuss the colour-coding system, showing every awareness of its subtlety and hierarchy, as children in a streamed school do of their classes, however cunningly devised the nomenclature. Their minimum ration per week is two cards, but they can do as many as they like. One glorious week Peter completed ten. When corrected by a friend for using the word 'sliva' for 'silver', he says, 'Yeah, that's my word for it.'

At 10.20a.m. Mr Barnes enters with a cardboard box.

Mr B.: Peter, do you want biscuits?
Peter: No, thank you, sir.

It is a kind of preliminary before break time at 10.30a.m. when most of the junior boys play football, most of the girls play ball games or wander around in pairs, arm in arm, and straying infants, untrained for such encounters, feel as if they are stumbling across a battleground.

As I write my notes in the classroom, two girls enter to practise their recorders and vehemently discuss which note is E and which G. I escape such controversy and talk in the staff room over coffee with a researcher from the National Foundation for Educational Research (NFER), who is monitoring teacher language and classroom control techniques, using chest microphones and his own observations to record the data. This reminds me that I have yet to hear any teacher utter any rebuke or to see any children criminally engaged. All of them, so far, appear to have been usefully and lawfully occupied.

180

After break the classroom fills up again and Peter and Kevin enter discussing their game of football, one side apparently having scored twenty-two goals. If only England were so adventurous!

Peter collects a sheet of paper from a tray in order to copy out the results of a science experiment he undertook the previous week. His final version is shown in Figure 6.1. The word omitted from the penultimate line is 'room'.

Various activities are going on around the room. Sixteen children are grouped around Mr Barnes, looking at a graph; two children in a corner are doing maths work; one girl is using washer discs as an aid in her maths corrections; two boys are working on a science experiment. From time to time children discuss their tasks with each other: 'What do we have to do?' ... 'How many have you got wrong?' ... 'Is this one easy or hard?' ... Learning is a participatory affair, a social, rather than a lonely, pursuit. 'Anyone can cheat at this', says one girl. 'I know', says another, 'but Sir said he'd trust us.'

<u>my experiment</u>

1. Air does weigh Something because me and Robert Cheadle did an experiment to see if air did weigh anything, and it did. We weighed an empty balloon, and an empty margarine carton on a balance beam until they were equal by putting plasticene on the empty balloon end.
So when it was equal we blew the balloon up and tied the end up with string.
And when we let it go the balloon was the heaviest so we put sand in the margarine carton to balance the beam. So when they were even there was about one gramme of sand in the margarine carton
So the air in the balloon weighed about one gramme.
2. The air in an ordinary weighs about the same as a bag of coal.

Figure 6.1

Peter continues to write slowly and carefully. Two children near him are discussing Christmas presents. One is having an electric guitar and the other an organ. Peter tells them that his mum and dad would never be able to afford those as they had just bought a carpet. There is no sense of loss or envy in his voice; it is merely a statement of fact.

The copying exercise takes sixteen minutes in all and the completed sheet is put in a wire basket for the teacher's attention later. Such a system permits more flexibility than an exercise book, but children collect together their best monthly pieces of work in a cumulative folder which stays with them throughout their school careers. They take it with them when they move on to secondary school.

Mr Barnes is now called out by a colleague experiencing tape-recorder problems. However, the children continue to work in their teacher's absence. A moment later he is back to carry on with studying the graph.

Peter wanders about for a minute or so, contemplating his next task, almost like a managing director thinking about his next piece of dictation. He watches the teacher for a moment and then is off to the library in search of his previous SRA card on the treasure trove. Perhaps such choice is an easy option for him.

He chuckles to himself as he rereads the card and appreciates a point in the story and before long has completed it. He is clearly able to work in a concentrated manner, whatever potential distraction is nearby. He takes the answer card but says to himself: 'I don't need it anyway. It's obvious what these are.' He marks his answers, scoring 8/10 and 32/33

At 11.35a.m. he returns the card to the box in the library and kneels on the floor colouring in his record sheet, reminiscent of a salesman marking up his successes, albeit on the floor. Again, he discusses the merits of different cards with one of the girls.

Peter: En I on silver twelve, Joanne?
Joanne: Yeah.
Jackie: Oh, bloody hell *(as she struggles with her card)*.

Then he chats with Tina who, he learns, does two or three cards per week and is on rose. If he can do five or six per week he will catch up with her. He questions Karen:

Peter: What's the most you've done in a week?
Karen: Three

Another little statistic to tuck away.

Peter now picks out his third card of the day, the last of the purple SRA cards (Purple 3, Lab IIa). This has a prose passage called, *Lawrence, Friend of the Arabs*, by R. J. Unstead, a very popular writer of history and religious education textbooks. Peter settles down to work on it.

Susan utters her thoughts out loud: 'How many threes in 121? Both flesh and spirit are weak. 'Oh, my God', she laments with the Psalmist, and inspiration comes through her mumbles. 'Oh, that's a good idea', she says to herself, and puts pencil to paper.

A handbell signals dinner time at twelve o'clock and no one stirs. Then, one by one, like actors at the end of a play, they pack away and go out to dine in family-type groups on faggots, peas and potatoes, plums and custard.

I chat with Peter for a while and he talks easily about his mum and dad, his brother aged 6 and sister 8, about football, cricket, quiz books and television. His Sunday schedule, with perhaps the 8.00 p.m. item omitted, would be many a schoolboy's dream. Here it is.

10.30 a.m.	Get up.
11.00	Breakfast
11.15	Playing 'up the park'.
1.30 p.m.	Dinner
2.00	Television (that is, soccer; a film; cartoons; a detective series).
5.30	Out again for football.
7.00	Tea.
7.30	Television.
8.00	Bath.
8.30	Television.
9.30	Bed.

Peter's eyes positively shine when we discuss his SRA Reading Laboratory activities. These are quite normal, he tells me, for a Monday morning and if he gets the chance later in the week he will return to them.

R.M.: You seem to like the Reading Lab, Peter *(laughs)*.

Peter: Yeah, I do.

R.M.: You're doing as many cards as you can, are you?

Peter: Yeah.

R.M.: Why are you doing that?

Peter: I don't know. I just want to finish first and I like doing it anyway.

(He is a satisfied customer in other respects, too, as his comments on the school indicate.)

R.M.: Now, Peter, tell me a bit about the school. What do you think of it?

Peter.: Very good.

R.M.: Yes. Why do you think it's very good?

Peter: We..,they take you for trips and everything. They don't lock the cameras away and they don't lock the tape recorders away. The televisions, they just keep them out for your use, like some of the schools they just lock them away.

R.M.: Mmm. Have you had any experience of that in a school?

Peter: Yeah. At me old school they just locked everything away. I didn't see the things. I hardly saw the things, but I knew we had some. But they just locked them away.

R.M.: I see ... Peter, tell me about your day at the old school. How was it different from this kind of day?

Peter: Well, we used to sit in the rows every day and we used to sit in the same old desks. Er ... we had stories all the time. Couldn't do the work we liked. Er ... nothing else really. They didn't let you wander around either like you can do here. That's it really.

R.M.: You think it's a good thing to be able to wander around?

Peter: Yeah.

R.M.: Why?

Peter: Well, I dunno ... it's wander ... wander around and see what you want to do. At our old school you had to wait and see what you had to do.

R.M.: Yes. You don't think that people waste time here?

Peter: Oh, a couple of 'em do. But, more or less, most of 'em don't. They get on with their work.

R.M.: Do you work harder here than you did at your old school?

Peter: Yeah.

R.M.: That's interesting, isn't it? You work harder even though you've got more freedom. Why is that then?

Peter: Because I want to go to a good senior school and er ... anyway I just like ... it's better work here altogether. They had a sort of Reading Lab but that was absolutely easy. It wasn't as hard as this and I like hard work.

R.M.: Yes. I got that impression of you working today. It's one of the things I've been interested in. You seem to be able settle down to your work and concentrate on it ...

Peter: Yeah.

R.M.: Even though there are a lot of other people about, all talking about different things. That doesn't seem to worry you at all.

Peter: No. Not really. I only leave that till play time.

Clearly, then, Peter is a serious-minded lad with an independent viewpoint, with some degree of self-analysis, and with strong motivation to succeed. At the same time, he is a balanced person, able to get on very well with his peers. He talks easily and with the confidence of someone who knows his own mind and is prepared to say what he thinks with firmness, but without arrogance. He is able to be objective about his own situation and to compare present with past experience. The school's credit points which he identifies would not all be every 10-year-old's choice: outside visits; accessibility of interesting equipment; choice of seating place and work; freedom to move about and act on your own initiative; use of a demanding reading laboratory.

Although it is dinner time now, a number of children are in the classroom, engaged in a variety of lawful pursuits. The margin between work time and play time, like the horizon on a hazy day, is not sharp. Two girls are playing the recorder; one adding on a calculator; one boy is smoothing a clay pot; three girls are doing maths; one girl is reading.

Then, at 1.30p.m. scheduled schooling begins again. Peter enters and, after having regained his SRA card, as a miser might his money box, he spends ten minutes crouching in the corridor with Kevin measuring with a metre rod distances children jump from stationary positions. Peter manages to win a small bet during this activity. A little group gathers around participants as the results are plotted. Peter settles down to his work card, sitting this time in the corridor at a table near the jumpers. Occasionally, he gets up to inspect jumping results. Lorna, a tall girl, makes a giant leap, much to the admiration of the onlookers and the gratification of the graph-makers.

One of the many interesting features about this class is how children occupy different seats throughout the day. They do not appear to be possessive over their territory (which provoked comment in Chapter 2) and I have yet to hear that evangelical call: 'Save us me seat!' Instead, they move to different places as the mood or activity takes them.

By 2.02p.m. Peter has checked his card and achieved 9/10 on one part and 31/33 on another. Such marks might indicate that he is not being challenged, as I felt could be the case with 8-year-old Lucy. Alternatively, he could be consolidating his position and gaining in confidence thereby. Certainly, we know from his remarks just recorded, that he feels he is working hard, and he is not a boy who likes to free-wheel. He is proud of his achievements and makes them clear to Mr Barnes, who checks through the work, explaining, as he does so, a point about suffixes.

The notion that school pupils must *constantly* be pushed to their limits would, if relentlessly pursued in an unthinking manner, breed a nation of neurotics. The cause of excellence, to which we all subscribe by virtue of our profession, may be better served by variations in pace, which allow time for thinking and for renewal. But this is not how we work as adults. Our effort, like our heartbeat, changes according to circumstance, to meet different demands. The heart should not pound all the time, but be in such good condition that it can respond to any reasonable call made upon it.

Having conquered the purple cards, Peter moves on to rose and a short piece by the science fiction writer, Arthur C. Clarke, *In Search of a Killer* (Rose 9, Lab IIa). However, he is diverted for a while and asked by one of his friends to participate in a science experiment. This involves being timed while running around the playground, with pre- and post-measurements of pulse rate. Four boys are working together on this project; Andrew has the stop watch. Peter duly performs on this now sunny but very cold day and is recorded as follows:

Pre-run pulse rate:	69
Post-run pulse rate:	79
Time taken for the run:	40 seconds

He is puffing heavily. Other children are recorded, including champion Lorna, who needs a re-run because the first measurement appeared to show a slower pulse rate *after* the run. They measure again. Peter races with her to begin with but, fifteen metres behind after sixty, retires from the unequal struggle. Lorna knocks three seconds off the record and registers a pulse rate of 98 (pre-run 87).

The boys discuss the results, continue with their measurements for a while, and then return upstairs to present their findings. Mr Barnes questions them:

Mr B.:   Did you use a stethoscope?
Pupil: No. Just by hand.
Mr B.:   What does it mean when your pulse rate increases?
         (Discussion follows.)
Pupil: I haven't got a pulse.

Mr Barnes shows the boys a stethoscope and explains how it works. They all discuss this and the significance of their pulse-rate findings.

This kind of approach to learning was indicated earlier in this chapter with the report of Peter's science experiment. Here it is seen at its most overt as 'learning by discovery'. At its best this is, paradoxically, a precise and disciplined activity. It has more in common with the thorough work of a detective, using reliable techniques to sift evidence and weigh information, rather than the haphazard and hopeful metal detector searching of a beach boy who dreams of finding buried treasure just below the surface. The stress is on the techniques of inquiry as much as their results; process as well as product.

The Plowden Report (1967) defines the concept and practice of discovery learning in clear terms:

In a number of ways it resembles the best modern university practice. Initial curiosity, often stimulated by the environment the teacher provides, leads to questions and to a consideration of what questions it is sensible to ask and how to find the answers. This involves a great exercise of judgement on the part of the teacher ... Essential elements are enquiry, exploration and first-hand experience ... If, as children become older, they jump to generalisations too readily from the results of a single experiment, the teacher should see that they repeat their experiments. By this means children's understanding of precision, reliability and the nature of evidence can be increased. Some enquiries will certainly lead children to books, and information picked up from books or from television will also provide starting points for enquiry. But if primary school science is confined to knowledge taken from books, the whole purpose of the study of this area of the curriculum will be lost. (para. 669)

Clearly, Peter and his contemporaries are engaged in this kind of learning. But he has been learning in other ways too. He has had experience so far today of working on his own; as one of a pair; as a member of a small group. He will shortly be a member of a class and, at the end of the afternoon, he will be in a competitive team structure during PE. In this way he is experiencing a variety of demands and learning how to conduct himself in a variety of contexts.

The class now prepares for the story, an activity which takes place daily, as a corporate involvement for all the children. The story is by Joan Aitken, *A Harp of Fishbones.* Having first asked the children what a harp is, what it looks like and how you play it, Mr Barnes goes on: 'You can have a very large harp, where you have to sit and you have to stand the harp on the floor. But some harps are small enough to hold in your hand. I think this story is about the sort of harp you could hold in your hand.'

In fact, the story is of an orphan girl, Nerryn, who is often punished by her employers for day-dreaming. She lives near a forest and works primarily for an old man, a would-be drunkard if he could afford it, called Timorash. Gradually, she collects information from a strange old woman, Saroon, about her dead father who had once played a harp of gold but had never returned from the strange kingdom beyond the forest. Nerryn determines to follow in her father's steps and she constructs a harp from the bones of large carp which she catches bodily while she is swimming in the mill pond. She journeys through the forest, charming the dangerous vultures *en route* with her playing. On arrival in the strange kingdom she releases from thrall all the frost-bound statuesque inhabitants who had been cursed by the goddess for their inordinate love of gold. 'I shall not come among you again until I am summoned by notes from a harp that is not made of gold, nor of silver, nor any precious metal, a harp that has never touched the earth but came from deep water, a harp that no man has ever played.' Nerryn has fulfilled the requirements of this curse and made possible the return of the goddess. There is singing and dancing in the kingdom as the little girl is welcomed by her grandfather, none other than the king. She makes a brief visit to the village in triumph and humility before returning to the kingdom, realizing that the old woman, Saroon, who had given her such useful advice and information, was, in reality, the incarnation of the spirit and music of the water.

Physically passive, but mentally active, Peter followed the narrative very carefully, smiling and laughing quietly at the parts he found amusing. There were two interruptions during the reading. One by the head teacher, who had come to collect some materials and who apologized for his intrusion. One by a parent who had come to collect her child's reading book.

Despite these two interruptions, which were both unobtrusive and quiet, by people sensitive to the situation, the children remained silent, held by the narrative and concentrating on it. Like the lovers of gold in the story, these children, too, were held in thrall. Of a rather less rigid variety, certainly, but, nevertheless, powerful.

Grouped informally, sitting on the floor around Mr Barnes's armchair, they followed the tale. One girl absent-mindedly plaited the hair of the girl in front of her; one boy handled a large fish jawbone. The fact that such an object was in the classroom at all is no coincidence. Like the stethoscope, it is here to relate to work in hand, to extend experience and make it more immediate, more vivid. It is further evidence, if that were needed, of Mr Barnes's planning, his imaginative awareness and professional involvement.

At 3.30p.m. the story finished and the children were reluctantly released from the fantasy which had gripped them and returned to the real world. In this instance, the world of PE. Normally, these two activities of the story and PE would be reversed in sequence but, on this occasion, the hall had been earlier occupied.

Six or seven boys and girls have forgotten their kit. Peter borrows a pair of blue shorts from Mr Barnes's cupboard and all go off to their cloakrooms to change.

Five minutes later the whole class has reassembled in the dining hall which doubles as a gym. It contains a piano, rostrum blocks, climbing frames, benches, buck, balls, hoops, a hot-air balloon (awaiting a good day for launching), an overhead projector, a record player, a needlework exhibition. There is no need, however, to thread one's way through this equipment, since the hall is large and light and has ample space in the middle for movement.

The children run round clockwise, then anti-clockwise. They jump up high, then crawl low. They hop high, then, like hiccuping crabs, nearer the floor. They leap over high (imaginary) fences; they burrow through earthbound (imaginary) tunnels. They move; freeze; move again. All seem to enjoy the contrasts and variety of these preliminary warm-up exercises. Peter, certainly, is fully involved and reasonably co-ordinated.

Next comes team work. Four teams are self-chosen, very quickly indeed, and each stands in line preparing to pass a ball from front to back, alternately over heads and under legs. Peter is situated half-way back in his team of eight, enjoying the activity and relating well to the other team members. This game over, the balls are dispensed with and, beginning with the front member of each team, each boy or girl moves down the line, climbing over and under each alternate child. Confusion reigns. Teacher explains. Confusion again. Peter's team resorts to cheating, the last refuge of the bewildered.

Finally, four teams again, with footballs to be tossed by each facing team leader to each boy and girl in turn and rolled by them back under the tunnel of legs of those in front to the team leader. Each member of the team acts as leader at some point.

At 4.00p.m. the bell sounds with the teams still busy. Six minutes later they finish and prepare to go home, a good time had by all. The lack of a clear demarcation line here at the end is curiously appropriate. There is no sense of occasion as school day ends and home life begins. The two worlds, in Peter's experience, have never been vary far apart anyway.

Sequel 1   Primary Science

Science is characterized by the method of working, that is, by using first-hand experiences to encourage children to think logically and systematically and in developing attitudes such as open-mindedness and critical reasoning, rather than being concerned only with subject content. Whether an activity such as Peter and his friends counting their pulse rates could be described as science rather than mathematics or PE depends very much on the questions asked as well as the context. Teachers can stimulate children's interest by contriving situations which arouse curiosity, asking questions which challenge them to investigate relevant problems and controlling the progression by structuring the discovery process. Table 1 gives some examples of questions which could be asked at different stages in the investigation and according to its purpose.

Table (2) shows how science work can change its emphasis as children gain experience and maturity.

Table 1

Questioning in Science Skills	Types of question/purpose	Examples
* **observation** - using appropriate senses	attention-focusing	Can you feel/hear your pulse? ... where?
* **comparison** – similarities and differences	comparison – help children to order and classify observation and data	Is the strength of the pulse the same in different parts of the body?/ for different people? Did Peter run faster than Andrew?
estimation and measurement	counting/measuring	How many times do you think/does your pulse beat in a minute?
* **sorting and classification**	classifying - useful in concept development	Can you group these together? ... Girls/Boys (on what criteria?)
* **prediction**	applying previous experience to a new situation	What do you think will happen to your pulse as you run?

Table 1   (continued)

Questioning in Science Skills	Types of question/purpose	Examples
making fair tests	reasoning – controlling variables	Is it fair to compare Lorna's pulse rate with Peter's? Did they have the same pulse rate at rest? Did they run the same distance? Did Peter run faster than Lorna?
looking for patterns and relationships	generalizing	Do all the children's pulse rates increase after running (exercise)? Is there a relationship between pulse and breathing rate?
drawing conclusions	reasoning	Why do you think your pulse rate increased?
critical thinking	reasoning – making judgements	How could we make the balance ... more accurate? Sensitive?
problem solving	test ideas/design experiments	Can you find a way to slow down your pulse?

* especially appropriate for infants

Table 2   Some suggestions for a Progression in Science Skills from Nursery Infant to Junior Level

	(Younger children – mainly) *qualitative* (descriptive methods)	(Older children – more) *quantitative* (analytical and evaluative methods)
Observation	Using sensory experience to explore the attributes and properties of living and non-living things, natural and man-made, (e.g. fruits and vegetables, containers.)	Extend sensory experience by using lens, microscope to look at detail, parts of objects, texture of materials, (e.g. mini beasts, leaves, fibres, crystals.) Use materials as well as objects, introduce names and descriptive vocabulary (e.g. 'symmetrical' 'hollow'.
Comparison	Ask questions to focus attention on colour, shape, size and texture. Opposites, (e.g. toys)	Use arbitrary and then standard measures. Use estimation, actual and approximation (e.g. strings – in relation to pitch)

Table 2   (continued)

(Younger children – mainly) *qualitative* (descriptive methods)	(Older children – more) *quantitative* (analytical and evaluative methods)
Measuring Discriminate between sounds high/low, loud/soft etc. (e.g. home-made musical instruments). Look at things from different angles, use prepositions to describe position, e.g. inside, outside the classroom, above/below the ground, on the top/bottom of water (floating/sinking)	Length → depth, height, distance weight area e.g. hands, feet (e.g. to break a strip of wood) Time ↘ Volume (e.g. lungs) ↘ Force Pressure (e.g. to move a load on a bridge.) ↘Temperature Speed (e.g. inside/out- (e.g. toy cars side classroom on ramp) air/water (pond))
Focus attention on one sense at a time by exclusion of others (e.g. use blindfold, nose-clip in tasting foods.) Use comparative adjectives e.g. hard, harder, hardest, → (e.g. materials-wood samples)	(in relation to experiments, in controlling variables, weather recording etc.) Use of simple then more complex scales. Ordering observations by pre- dicting, then measuring, e.g. weight density
Sorting Use sets and intersecting matrices classification sub-sets sets	
1 criterion → several → alternative → (e.g. shapes-logi criteria methods blocks or colour) (e.g. buttons, e.g. colour, powders) shape, size, dissolving	use of identifi- cation keys, punch cards, tree diagrams, data bases (e.g. mini beasts no. of legs. metals/ non-metals.)
Experi- menting Making predictions in simple situations, where only a few alternatives, → and results can be seen clearly. (e.g. will it sink/float?) (Based on intuition/previous experience: Heavy/Light	Stating hypotheses which can be tested by experiment and proved or disproved easily. (e.g. A tin foil boat will float – because it has a large surface area and its shape displaces more than its own weight of water).
Making fair tests →	Controlling/Separating [variables] (e.g. bouncing
Alter only one factor at a time, e.g. size.	balls drop from same height, drop on same surface, compare material, hollow/solid etc.)

Table 2   (continued)

	(Younger children – mainly) *qualitative* (descriptive methods)		(Older children – more) *quantitative* (analytical and evaluative methods)	
Recording	Mainly talking, visual, drawing whole item		More detailed drawing, labelling parts	Apparatus drawing, diagrams, symbols. Tabulation of data in matrices
Looking for patterns	Blockgraphs e.g. eye colour	→ Simple tabulation →		Histograms e.g. height, weight, children in the class.
			Barcharts (e.g. traffic surveys)	Line graphs (e.g. seedling growth, cooling curve
	Simple symbols (e.g. weather recording maps.)			Pie charts (e.g. bird surveys – food preference)

Discussion between children and with the teacher is a very important part of learning process, especially in developing understanding of concepts and the meaning of words in relation to actual objects and situations. Science activities can provide valuable opportunities to develop vocabulary and explore the use of language and to apply mathematical skills in real life contexts to sort, measure and to display results graphically. Recording can sometimes inhibit exploration; it is not necessary to get children to write down everything – only essential points and the actual data. The activity itself and talking is the most important contribution science can make to learning. In order for children to see patterns and relationships from data it is suggested that teachers of infants or less able children use a combination of pictorial methods, flash cards showing key words, observations etc. and tables and graphs with older or more able children. Even able juniors can be discouraged by having to write up every experiment. It is probably best to do a 'model write-up' using the following headings:

(Before the investigation.)
(1) *What we want to find out*/Title.
(2) *What we need*/List of equipment

(After the investigation)
(1) *What we did*/Method (including a drawing)

(2) *What happened*/Table of results
(3) *What we found out*/Conclusion

Once the children get used to this approach they can quite quickly adapt this recording method to other investigations. Sometimes a piece of personal or free writing may be preferred. In any case, it is probably too much to expect children to record work in any detail or depth in the same lesson as the activity. Language lessons could well be used for discussing science work or as 'exercises' in descriptive or transactional writing. If teachers use a thematic approach, that is, groups of children work on different, but related, activities there is also much scope for children to report on their work to the rest of the class, using a wide range of communication skills including oral, written and visual methods. The test of whether real science is going on in the classroom is to ask:

(1) Has the teacher enriched children's environment for learning and encouraged children to develop attitudes of responsibility, perseverance and independence which support scientific enquiry?
(2) Have the children been actively involved in exploring? Have they enjoyed themselves and do they want to go on finding out?

Books for further reference

Schools Council (1972–1975) *Science 5-13* series as a resource, and 'With Objectives in Mind', for the process of science (London: Macdonald.)

Schools Council (1982) *Learning Through Science* Formulating a School Policy (for organization, assessment, record keeping) and Workcards on *Science 5/13* main themes Science Resources (London: Macdonald.)

County of Avon (1981–1986) *Primary Science Working Papers 1–6* (for concepts, skills and attitudes, flowcharts) (Maths, Science & Technology Centre, Bishop Road, Bristol B57 8LS.)

Hayes, M. (ed.) (1982) *Starting Primary Science* (For observation skills) (London: Edward Arnold.)

Harlen, W. (ed.) (1985) *Primary Science: Taking the Plunge* (For questioning technique) (London: Heinemann.)

Hargrave, E. and Brooks, J. (1986) *Science World* (For questioning, prediction, fair testing and developing science from topic work) (London: Longman.)

Raper, G. and Stringer, J. (1987) *Encouraging Primary Science* (An overview of all aspects) (London: Cassell.)

Sequel 2   *Classroom Organization and Teaching Observation*

There are hundreds of observation schedules. Many of them involve boxes to be ticked and resulting matrices to be analysed. What is offered here is a checklist of questions to act as prompts to observation.

The checklist can be used, selectively, by any experienced teacher who observes a colleague. This is presently a fairly rare occurrence, but could become more common under the new In-Service arrangements. It may also be used by student teachers who, as part preparation for teaching practice/school experience, observe a class whom they expect eventually to teach. This is hardly disinterested observation.

Some of the sections, notably those on equipment and language, need to be used over a period of days or weeks since they are likely to be fairly time consuming and to involve considerable follow-up. Many of the supplementary questions are more appropriate for discussion than writing.

Classroom Environment

(1) Draw a plan of your own classroom or the classroom you are studying, to show chairs and tables, curriculum areas (for example, art; science), equipment including furniture.
     Whatdoestheplantellyouabouttheteachingstylesintheroom and about the curriculum organization?
(2) What displays are around the room? Which of these are semi-permanent? Why? Which are changing? Why?
(3) Which children currently have their work on display? Why?

(4) Does the classroom environment reflect a competitive spirit or a co-operative atmosphere, or are there aspects of both? Which do you prefer and why?

(5) What evidence is there of cross-curricular work? How do you regard such work?

(6) What evidence is there of 'basic' skills work? What is your own approach in this respect?

(7) What evidence is there of conformity to a national curriculum? What is your attitude towards this concept?

(8) What indications are there in the classroom of a world outside (and perhaps inside, too,) which is culturally diverse? What indications, in your view, should there be?

(9) What books are in the room and what underlying messages might they convey about the nature of reading? (A pleasure or a grind? Linear or haphazard? Chained or on open access?)

(10) The final question, bearing in mind the time of the academic year when your observation takes place:
Which of these words describe the room?
– warm; welcoming; interesting; lively; colourful;
– dull; unimaginative; restricting; uniform; unstimulating.

Teaching Observation

EQUIPMENT

(1) Which of the following were used? Chalkboard; text book; reference book; work sheet; handout; exercise book; paper; general work book; map; tape recorder; overhead projector; television; video tape recording; computer; film; filmstrip; slides; photographs; pictures; objects; other specialist equipment? Were any, in your view, used unsatisfactorily? Why do you think so?

(2) What procedures were followed for the distribution and collection of books. Were these satisfactory?

(3) What equipment had the boys and girls brought with them? What provision was there for those without?

(4) Where were new exercise books or sheets of paper kept and how were they issued?

(5) Where were the chalkboard cleaner and spare chalk kept?

(6) (For follow-up later): What other equipment and books does the school possess which needs checking on?

ROUTINES

(1) Were the children required to put up their hands before speaking? Did this invariably happen? Do you think it should?
(2) Were the children allowed to move freely about the room during the lesson? Should they be allowed to do this?
(3) How did the children sit – in rows/groups/other? Why? What do you favour?
(4) Did the children work as a class, or in pairs, or in small groups? How were these groupings determined – by teacher/task/friendship/ability? Why? When in your view, did they work best?
(5) What other standard routines did you notice?
(6) Were there any occasions when the normal routine appeared to be disrupted?

MANAGEMENT

(1) How did the teacher keep order?
    (a) By personality and relationship with the class?
    (b) By containing the children with work and/or the lesson's intrinsic interest?
    (c) By speaking quietly to awkward individuals?
    (d) By threats and/or shouting and/or punishments?
    (e) By removal from the classroom?
        Which aspects of behaviour were not tolerated by the teacher?
(2) How would you describe the teacher's relationship with the class and the teaching style used?
    (a) Firm but friendly?
    (b) Strict and authoritarian?
    (c) *Laissez-faire?*
    (d) Democratic?
    (e) Weak and ineffectual?
    (f) Competent but dull?
(3) How would you describe the motivation of the class?

(a) High level and sustained?
(b) Reasonable?
(c) Reluctant?
(d) Sporadic?
(e) Non-existent?
What methods do you feel (would) best motivate this class? Which boys and girls, if any, were clearly unmotivated?

(4) Did the teacher address the whole class by its name (for example, '2A' or 'Second Years')? Was this appropriate?
How did the children address the teacher: Miss; Mrs; Sir; Madam; Mr; Mate; by name?

(5) Did the teacher stand at the front of the room and/or move around, working with individuals, and/or sit at, or on, the desk?

(6) How was the class dismissed?
(a) What words did the teacher use?
(b) Did the children leave a row or a group at a time, or altogether?
(c) Did the lesson finish punctually?

(7) In what frame of mind do you think the boys and girls would be ready for their next piece of classwork?

LESSON STRUCTURE

(1) What appeared to be the teacher's objectives? Did s/he mention them to the class at any point? Do you think they were fulfilled?

(2) What, precisely, do you think, was learned, and by whom? How was assessment of the work carried out?
(a) By marking or written pieces?
(b) By testing?
(c) By noting oral contributions?
(d) By judgement of a picture, painting, model or design?

(3) What was the sequence of the lesson? (For instance, was it: exposition, discussion, writing?)
Was there a summary and/or conclusion at the end of the lesson?
Was 'the lesson' merely part of on-going work, with no perceptible beginning or end?

(4)   What balance was there between class/group listening and class/group activity?
(5)   How was factual information conveyed?
    (a)   By writing on the chalkboard or using the overhead projector?
    (b)   By worksheet or handout?
    (c)   By dictation?
    (d)   By reference or text book?
    (e)   By note-making or note-taking?
    (f)   By some other method?
    Which of these were most appropriate?
(6)   What, precisely, were the children required to do?
(7)   What work, if any, did the boys and girls initiate?
(8)   Were children of all abilities being catered for?
(9)   Was the teacher working alone with the class, or co-operatively with colleagues, in some form of team-teaching?

LANGUAGE

(1)   How did the teacher greet the children?
    What were the first words to begin the teaching session?
(2)   What were the approximate proportions of teacher talk/class or group talk/one-to-one talk?
(3)   Could the teacher be understood at all times?
    How did you react to the teacher's choice of words, volume, speed, accent, mannerisms?
(4)   What were the approximate proportions of open and closed questions?
(5)   Were there any jokes? Were they good ones?
(6)   Were there different levels of question, demanding:
    (a)   Factual recall?
    (b)   Re-ordering of information or experience?
    (c)   Speculation?
    (d)   Evaluation or judgement?
(7)   How did the teacher encourage and give praise?
    What were some of the actual words used?
(8)   How did s/he rebuke and complain?
    What were some of the actual words used?
(9)   How were new words introduced? Were they:
    (a)   Highlighted, defined and discussed?
    (b)   Written on the board?

(c)   Looked at from the spelling point of view?

(10)   Was the classroom noise that of a working atmosphere? How do you judge?

Final question as Summary.

(11)   What, as an observer, did you learn, which will modify your own teaching in future?

Sequel 3   Teacher Training Tasks

Chapter 6 Peter

(1)   Discuss Peter's classroom environment and its potential. Which of the first ten questions in the Sequel 'Class room Organization and Teaching Observation' could you reasonably answer about this room?

(2)   In what ways do teacher-pupil relationships in Peter's class appear to differ from those discussed elsewhere in this book?

(3)   Is Peter intellectually stretched during the day, or free-wheeling?

(4)   What are the advantages and disadvantages in the children being able to choose their own sequence and place of work, as well as some of their tasks?

(5)   How far would you agree with my comments on SRA work cards (both in this chapter and in Chapter 4)?

(6)   What seems to be the advantages and disadvantages of materials such as Ginn 360?

(7)   Judging by the story, 'A Harp of Fishbones', what do you believe can be the value of fantasy for such children as Peter?

(8)   The Sequel on 'Primary Science' seeks to match Peter's experience against certain skill categories. Use the checklist in the Sequel and measure it against any piece of science teaching you observe or are involved with.

(9)   Use the checklist in the Sequel on 'Classroom Organization and Teaching Observation' against which to measure any classroom you know and any piece of teaching you observe.

Bibliography and Further Reading

Armstrong, M. (1980) *Closely Observed Children* (London: Writers and Readers, in association with Chameleon).

Ashton, P. *et al.* (1975) *The Aims of Primary Education* (London: Macmillan).

Ashton, P. (1981) 'The aims of primary education revisited' in B. Simon and J. Willcocks (eds) *Research and Practice in the Primary School* (London: Routledge & Kegan Paul).

Barnes, D. *et al.* (1969) *Language, the Learner and the School* (Harmondsworth: Penguin).

Barnes, D. (1976) *From Communication to Curriculum* (Harmondsworth: Penguin).

Barrett, G. H. (1986) *Starting School: An Evaluation of the Experience* (London: AMMA).

Bassey, M. (1978) *Nine Hundred Primary Teachers* (Slough: National Federation for Educational Research).

Bennett, S. N. (1976) *Teaching Styles and Pupil Progress* (London: Open Books).

Blenkin, G. M. and Kelly, A. V. (eds) (1983) *The Primary Curriculum in Action: A Process Approach to Educational Practice* (London: Harper & Row).

Blyth, W. (1984) *Development, Experience and Curriculum in Primary Education* (London: Croom Helm).

Brandling, R. (1978) *Festive Occasions in the Primary School* (London: Ward Lock Educational).

Britton, J. L. (1970) *Language and Learning* (Harmondsworth: Penguin).

Bullock Report (1975) *A Language for Life* (London: HMSO).

Burgess, R. G. (ed.) (1985a) *Field Methods in the Study of Education* (Lewes: Falmer Press).

Burgess, R. G. (ed.) (1985b) *Strategies of Educational Research: Qualitative Methods* (Lewes: The Falmer Press).

Campbell, r. (1985) *Developing the Primary School Curriculum* (London: Holt, Rinehart & Winston).

Croll, P. (1986) *Systematic Classroom Observation* (Lewes: Falmer Press).

Davies, B. (1982) *Life in the Classroom and Playground: The Accounts of Primary School Children* (London: Routledge & Kegan Paul).

Dearden, R. F. (1968) *The Philosophy of Primary Education* (London: Routledge & Kegan Paul).

Dearden, R. F. (1976) *Problems in Primary Education* (London: Routledge & Kegan Paul).

Delamont, S. (1983) *Interaction in the Classroom* (London: Methuen).

Delamont, S.(ed.)(1987)*The Primary School Teacher*(Lewes:Falmer Press).

Department of Education and Science (1972) *Movement: Physical Education in the Primary Years* (London: HMSO).

Department of Educational Science (1985) *The Curriculum from 5–16*, Curriculum Matters Series 2 (London: HMSO).

Dewey, J. (1966) *Democracy and Education* (New York: Free Press Education).

Fisher, R. (1987) *Problem Solving in Primary Schools* (Oxford: Basil Blackwell).

Ford Teaching Project (1975) *Ways of Doing Research in One's Own Classroom* (Norwich CARE: University of East Anglia).

Garvey, C. (1984) *Children's Talk* (London: Fontana).

Gloyn, S. and Frobisher, B. (1975) *Teaching Basic Skills to Infants*(London: Ward Lock).

Good, T. L. and Brophy, J. E. (1984) *Looking in Classrooms* (London: Harper & Row).

Harling, P. and Roberts, T. (1988) *Primary Mathematics Schemes. How to Choose and Use* (London: Hodder & Stoughton).

Hartley, D. (1985) *Understanding the Primary School: A Sociological Analysis* (London: Croom Helm).

Hilsum, S. and Cane, B. (1971) *The Teacher's Day* (Windsor: NFER).

Holt, J. (1967) *How Children Learn* (Harmondsworth: Penguin).

Holt, J. (1974) *Escape from Childhood* (Harmondsworth: Penguin).

Hopkins, D. (1985) *A Teacher's Guide to Classroom Research* (Milton Keynes: Open University Press).

Inner London Education Authority (1985) *Improving Primary Schools* (The Thomas Report) (London: ILEA).

Jackson, P. W. (1968) *Life in Classrooms* (New York: Holt, Rinehart & Winston).

Jennings, J. (1977) 'History and environmental studies', *Trends in Education* vol. 4, winter (London: HMSO).

King, R. (1977) *Education* (London: Longman).

King, R. (1978) *All Things Bright and Beautiful?* (New York: Wiley).

Lambert, I. M. (1976) *The Teaching of Reading* (Derby: Professional Association of Teachers).

Marsh, L. G. (1970a) *Alongside the Child* (London: A & C Black).

Marsh, L. G. (1970b) *Approach to Mathematics* (London: A & C Black).

Meadows, S. (1986) *Understanding Child Development* (London: Century Hutchinson).

Neill, A. S. (1939) *The Problem Teacher* (London: Herbert Jenkins).

Nixon, J. (1981) *A Teacher's Guide to Action Research* (London: Grant McIntyre).

Open University (1981) P234 *Curriculum in Action: An Approach to Evaluation*, Block 5, Observing Classroom Processes (Milton Keynes: Open University Press).

Parry, M. and Archer, H. (1975) *Two to Five* (London: Macmillan).

Perera, K. (1984) *Children's Writing and Reading* (Oxford: Blackwell).

Peters, R. S. (1966) *Ethics and Education* (London: Allen & Unwin).

Piaget, J. (1941) *The Child's Conception of Number* (London: Routledge & Kegan Paul).

Plowden Report (1967) *Children and Their Primary Schools* (London: HMSO).

Pumphrey, P. D. (1977) *Measuring Reading Abilities* (London: Hodder & Stoughton).

Ridgway, L. (1976) *Task of the Teacher in the Primary School* (London: Ward Lock Educational).

Sinclair, J. Mc H. and Coulthard, R. M. (1975) *Towards an Analysis of Discourse* (Oxford: OUP).

Stewart, J. (1986) *The Making of the Primary School* (Milton Keynes: Open University Press).

Stubbs, M. and Delamont, S. (1976) *Explorations in Classroom Observation* (London: Wiley).

Tizard, B. and Hughes, M. (1984) *Young Children Learning: Talking and Thinking at Home and at School* (London: Fontana).

Torbe, M. (1977) *Teaching Spelling* (London: Ward Lock Educational).

Tough, J. (1976) *Listening to Children Talking* (London: Ward Lock Educational).

Wade, B. (1986) *Stories for You* (Leeds: Arnold-Wheaton).

Walker, R. (1985) *Doing Research: A Handbook for Teachers* (London: Methuen).

Waller, W. (1932) *The Sociology of Teaching* (New York: Wiley).

Warnock Report (1978) *Special Educational Needs* (London: HMSO).

Waterland, L. (1985) *Read With Me* (Gloucester: Thimble Press).

Wells, G. (1987) *The Meaning Makers* (London: Hodder & Stoughton).

Woods, P. (1987) 'Becoming a junior: pupil development following transfer from infants', in A. Pollard (ed.) *Children and Their Primary Schools* (Lewes: Falmer Press).

Index

Name Index